10-9
GEN
9.99

D1027384

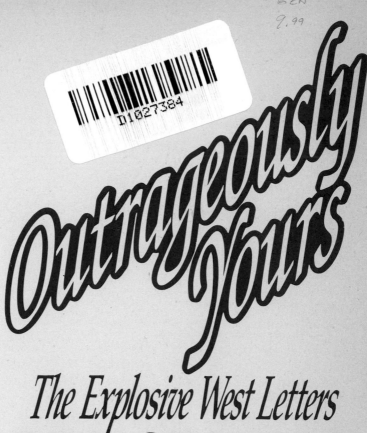

Outrageously Yours

The Explosive West Letters

BRUCE WEST

General
— PAPERBACKS —
Toronto, Canada

Copyright©1986 by Bruce West

All rights reserved. No part of this book may be reproduced
or transmitted in any form or by any means, electronic or
mechanical, including photography, recording or any
information storage and retrieval system, without permission
in writing from the publisher.

General Paperbacks edition published 1986

ISBN 0-7736-7122-6

Cover Design: Brant Cowie/Artplus Ltd.
Cover Illustration: Ken Suzana

Printed and bound in Canada

The author, a trainee construction labourer who resides in a sleepy seaside retirement town on the edge of nowhere, has selflessly assumed the daunting burden of establishing a vital link between the ordinary person and People of Consequence who exercise their influence on our everyday lives.

309-941 West 13th Avenue
Vancouver
British Columbia
V5Z 1P4

John Turner
PRIME MINISTER
House of Commons
OTTAWA
Ontario K1A 0A6

August 20th 1984

Dear Prime Minister,

In common with all concerned Canadians at this important crossroads in our political history, I am examining my conscience in order to determine the party most meritorious of my approbation in the forthcoming Federal Election.

I have long been a devout Liberal, and a fervent disciple of your predecessor, Pierre Trudeau, and I am therefore concerned that his successor should be a man of suitable standing and character in order to maintain an impressive leadership.

Therefore, in order to secure my continuing allegiance, I should like you to put my mind at rest over a couple of points regarding your personal credibility.

My first concern is that I gather you, Mr. Turner, are a Lawyer. Now, whilst I do not necessarily subscribe to the widely held view that the Legal profession is run for criminals, by criminals, I must confess that I am not entirely convinced that the level of scruples required to sustain a legal practice are appropriate to political leadership.

My second point is with regard to your somewhat disappointing mien when engaged in verbal dialogue with the media, public, and fellow politicians. I am concerned that your general inarticulation, reticence, and facial expression assume the characteristics one would expect of a schoolboy caught in the act of exposing his private parts in the girls changing room at Secondary School! Hardly the assertive composure one would expect from a man in your position.

I understand that you are also the Liberal candidate for Vancouver Quadra, and I should like assurance that the voters in this riding are being offered a sound prospect for their money. I hardly need to remind you that British Columbians are not men of the World by any stretch of the imagination, and I should not care to see their naivety presumed upon. My vote and support will be carefully gauged upon your ability to convince me that my misgivings are without foundation.

I look forward to your early assurances.

Yours sincerely,

Bruce West

309-941 West 13th Avenue
Vancouver
British Columbia
V5Z 1P4

John Turner
PRIME MINISTER
House of Commons
OTTAWA
Ontario K1A 0A6

September 5th 1984

Dear Mr. Turner,

Just a quiet note of condolence regarding the fate of the Liberal Party yesterday, and a cordial congratulation on your securing Vancouver Quadra.

Pay no heed to the bovine critics who say that your leadership is wholly responsible for the crushing humiliation of all the Party has stood for over the years - I am confident that with a few months of careful grooming, you will find your public image improved beyond all recognition. Incidentally, if you read between the lines of my letter dated August 20th, you may care to reflect that my advice therein contains more than a grain or two of truth.

On a more serious point, appertaining to the responsibility of the National Press at this sensitive time, the 'Globe & Mail' (August 25th, page E8) in a disturbing book review by Jeffrey Simpson, states that you are a devout Catholic who at one stage considered priesthood.

Personally, my view is that whether a man is inclined toward extremist religious practice or not is entirely his own business (the Ayatollah Khomeini hasn't done too badly from his particular persuasion!) but the woolly-minded voter may not be as broad minded as you and I. Nonetheless you may care to take the Globe to task over this untimely piece.

With all best wishes for the future.

Yours sincerely,

Bruce West

P.S. Could you oblige with an autographed photo? Many thanks.

309-941 West 13th Avenue
Vancouver
British Columbia
V5Z 1P4

September 21st 1984

John Turner
House of Commons
OTTAWA
Ontario
K1A 0A6

Dear Mr. Turner,

     I am astounded that you have not had the common civility to reply to my letters dated August 20th and September 5th.

     Is this irresponsible attitude typical of the appreciation a devoted Party campaigner might expect of his Leader?

     Get a grip on yourself my good man!

     I look forward to your early apology and reply.

                    Yours sincerely,

                    Bruce West

HOUSE OF COMMONS
CHAMBRE DES COMMUNES
CANADA

Office of the Leader of the Opposition
Cabinet du Chef de l'Opposition

Ottawa, Ontario
K1A 0A6

November 7, 1984

Mr. Bruce West
309-941 West 13th Avenue
Vancouver, British Columbia
V5Z 1P4

Dear Mr. West:

On behalf of the Right Honourable John N. Turner, I wish to acknowledge receipt of your letters of September 5th and September 21st. I apologize for the delay in acknowledging your correspondence.

As you requested, I am pleased to send a photograph of Mr. Turner.

Sincerely,

Elizabeth Coburn
Special Assistant

Encl.

309-941 West 13th Avenue
Vancouver
British Columbia
V5Z 1P4

Geoffrey Stevens
Managing Editor
The Globe & Mail
444 Front Street W.   September 7th 1984
Toronto
Ontario M5V 2S9

Dear Mr. Stevens,

        I write as a concerned political analyst regarding the
book review in the Globe & Mail (August 25th page E8) wherein
Jeffrey Simpson states that Prime Minister John Turner is a
committed Catholic who at one stage considered priesthood.

        No doubt you would agree with me that a man's <u>private</u>
religious persuasion is his own business, however extreme or bizarre
it may appear. The Canadian voting public however, cannot be
assumed to be as broad minded as you and I, and I must state
therefore that I think the publishing of this review during
Mr. Turner's campaign is grossly irresponsible.

        I note incidentally that no such potentially damaging
reviews on the lives of Mr. Mulroney or Mr. Broadbent were
carried by the Globe during the election campaign, to balance
any influence on the electorate.

        I have kept in close personal contact with Mr. Turner
throughout his campaign, and I know that although he is not the
sort of man to demand a satisfactory explanation from your paper,
there is no doubt that a written apology would be the least one
could expect in the circumstances.

        I await sir, your immediate reply.

                              Yours sincerely,

                              Bruce West

The Globe and Mail

OFFICE OF THE
MANAGING EDITOR

444 FRONT STREET WEST
TORONTO, M5V 2S9

September 21, 1984

Bruce West
309-941 West 13th Avenue
Vancouver, B.C.
V5Z 1P4

My Dear Mr. West:

Your letter of 7 September could scarcely have been
more to the point. I concur wholeheartedley with
your assessment of the receptivity of the masses.
The public is not - and could not reasonably be
expected to be - as broad-minded as you and I when
it comes to accepting the bizarre private religious
convictions of our leaders.

Jeffrey Simpson did state that John Turner is a
committed Catholic who once considered entering the
priesthood. I have scoured the files. I have searched
every nook and cranny of the computer, but I can find
no equivalent attack on any politician of the Progressive
Conservative or even New Democratic party stripe. In
neither of those parties did we uncover (I suspect we
may not even have endeavored to uncover) a single
Anabaptist or Zoroastrian. Who knows how many Swabians,
let alone zooflagellates, may be lurking in the
corridors of our new Government.

Your reprimand is well taken. I trust you will show
the same commendable dispatch in drawing any future
lapses to my attention.

I am,
Your Ob't Servant,

Geoffrey Stevens

/ss

309-941 West 13th Avenue
Vancouver
British Columbia
V5Z 1P4

The Globe & Mail
444 Front Street West
Toronto
Ontario   September 29th 1984
M5V 2S9

For the attention of Geoffrey Stevens
<u>Managing Editor</u>

Dear Mr. Stevens,

        I am deeply moved by your letter dated September 21st,
not only because it serves as a profound testimonial to the
ultimate dedication one expects of a Leader of the Free Press,
but because outside our respective professional obligations we
both strive toward the common goal of a political machine free
from obsolete doctrinarianism.

        Your sober approbation of one's concern over the doubtful
elements infiltrating the corridors of power in this fair country
inspires one to a renewed sense of patriotism.

        You may rest assured that my people at this end will be
maintaining a critical watch on matters political as you suggest,
and any sightings of Muggletonian, Druid, Christadelphian, Jansenist,
or like convocation, will be immediately forwarded to your good
office for expert analysis.

                              Yours gratefully

                              Bruce West

Brian Mulroney
Progressive Conservative Party
House of Commons
OTTAWA
Ontario K1A 0A2

309-941 West 13th Avenue
Vancouver
British Columbia
V5Z 1P4

August 23rd 1984

Dear Mr. Mulroney,

If the polls are to be relied upon, it would appear likely that our next government will be formed by your Party.

In the past, I have normally favoured the Liberals as being fairly sound people, but with the departure of Mr. Trudeau, I feel sure that their path to obscurity will be swift under the lack-lustre 'leadership' of the appalling John Turner.

Thus, I am bound to say that providing you are able to satisfy me regarding a couple of issues, the Progressive Conservatives may count upon my enthusiastic support in the future.

I have seen your performance on the television and in the newspapers Mr. Mulroney, and there is no doubt that you are an eloquent speaker, sharp, positive, and forthright - well done!

However, I should very much like you to make your position quite clear regarding Conservative policy toward Ronald Reagan, the ex-film star and now U.S.A. President.

Those of us who are heavily committed to psychological research are in little doubt that Mr. Reagan is a megalomaniac, intent on early destruction of all countries in the Eastern Bloc.

Like yourself, Mr. Reagan is of Irish origin, not necessarily a hindrance in itself - a man cannot be held responsible for his ethnic origins, but I have spent some time in Ireland studying the people, and it is abundantly clear that the native physiology lacks certain attributes that one would consider essential in responsible political leadership.

If elected next month, I should also like assurances that you will not emulate the policies of your counterparts in Britain, where the Pound Sterling is at an all time low, and unemployment is at an all time high.

My allegiance to the Progressive Conservatives will hinge on your satisfactory comment regarding these points.

I look forward to hearing from you.

Yours sincerely,

Bruce West

CANADA

PRIME MINISTER • PREMIER MINISTRE

Ottawa, K1A 0A2
September 27, 1984

Mr. Bruce West,
Apartment 309,
941 West 13th Avenue,
Vancouver, British Columbia.
V5Z 1P4

Dear Mr. West,

I wish to acknowledge and thank you for your letter
of August 23.

The people of Canada voted in a decisive manner for
our Party because they had confidence in the ability of my
colleagues and me to govern effectively and responsibly. We
take seriously the mandate given to us by the electorate and
I can assure you we will act in Canada's best interests at
all times.

Again, I appreciate your writing and I hope you
will keep me informed of your views in the months ahead.

With every good wish,

Yours sincerely,

309-941 West 13th Avenue
Vancouver
British Columbia
Canada V5Z 1P4

President Ronald Reagan
The White House
Washington D.C.
20500
U.S.A.

September 6th 1984

Dear Mr. Reagan,

Turn the other cheek to the woolly minded leftist
liberals who jump down your throat at the merest jocular threat
to bomb the Russians. I speak for a large majority of clear
thinking Canadians when I affirm our support of your commendable
policy that all communist aggressors should be wiped off the face
of the Earth, in spite of the extreme likelihood of terminal
global annihilation.

More power to your elbow; North America and the Free World
waits with bated breath for your next inspired gem of unparalleled
diplomatic genius.

By now of course, you will be aware that Brian Mulroney
(I believe you have already exchanged pleasantries) is to be our
next Prime Minister. I feel sure that you will get on well with
Mr. Mulroney, who in these early stages is obviously not a Great
Leader like yourself, but he shapes up well.

It would be an exaggeration for me to claim to be close
to Mr. Mulroney, but we do exchange private correspondence from
time to time on various matters of National importance, and I can
commend him to you most highly, in spite of his relative inexperience.

May I take this opportunity to wish you well in your
personal election campaign, and if at any time I can assist you to
your just deserts, I am at your service!

Yours sincerely,

Bruce West

309-941 West 13th Avenue
Vancouver
British Columbia
V5Z 1P4

Brian Mulroney
Progressive Conservative Party
House of Commons
OTTAWA
Ontario K1A 0A2

September 6th 1984

Dear Mr. Mulroney,

Many congratulations on the Tory landslide, due in no small part to your eloquent speech writers and omnipresent wife, Mila.

Cynics among us may claim the lack of opposition offered by the retarded performance of Mr. Turner, and the blustering Mr. Broadbent (NDP), made for an easy victory, but I for one am not unimpressed by the outcome, and anticipate early adherence to all the Progressive Conservative promises.

I have incidentally, recently enjoyed an exchange of private letters with the American President, Ronald Reagan, and have in the course of same, reassured him as to your suitability for the leadership of this great country.

I do hope that my assurances to the President will stand the test of time.

If I can be of further service, I am at your command.

Yours sincerely,

Bruce West

CANADA

PRIME MINISTER · PREMIER MINISTRE

Ottawa, K1A 0A2
November 9, 1984

Dear Bruce,

I would like to thank you so much for your very kind words of congratulations and best wishes on our Party's victory in the recent election. I was delighted to receive your letter.

The overwhelming mandate which the Canadian people gave us on September 4 is a responsibility we will treat with care and dignity. Our new government will immediately set to work to restore prosperity and opportunity to this great country in full recognition of the tremendous encouragement we have so recently received from the people of Canada.

The work, effort and convictions of a great many people were necessary to make this victory possible. These next few months will be a challenging time for us as we begin to establish the government which Progressive Conservatives across this country have worked so hard to make happen.

Thank you again for your letter. It was a pleasure to hear from you.

With every good wish,

Yours sincerely,

Mr. Bruce West,
    Apartment 309,
        941 West 13th Avenue,
            Vancouver, British Columbia.
                V5Z 1P4

309-941 West 13th Avenue
Vancouver
British Columbia
Canada V5Z 1P4

President Ronald Reagan
The White House
Washington D.C.
U.S.A.
20500

October 10th 1984

Dear Mr. Reagan,

I am both shocked and disappointed!

I wrote to you on September 6th expressing my admiration
for your courageous approach to the severe global problems confronting
the civilised peoples of our two great countries, also putting to
paper my wishes for your sempiternal and cordial rapport with Brian
Mulroney, and to date I have not received the common courtesy of
a reply.

Is this the American way?

If we are to maintain a policy of improving relations, then
surely our mutual obligations must include fluid communication.

I have on my desk a letter from Mr. Mulroney, dated
September 27th, concerning various matters of state, in which he also
requests of me, "I hope you will keep me informed of your views in the
months ahead", and to this end I should certainly wish to be able to
include a line of encouragement concerning the combined efforts of
our two nations to at least demonstrate the ability to enjoy a
respectful interchange of letters.

I know that you in particular Mr. President, as an
equilibrist and Christian, personally deplore laxity of behaviour
in social intercourse, and I am assuming therefore that your failure
to reply to my letter is an isolated oversight.

I trust I may now look forward to your early missive.

Yours sincerely,

Bruce West

Note: No reply received. —Ed.

309-941 West 13th Avenue
Vancouver
British Columbia
V5Z 1P4

Ed Broadbent
New Democratic Party
House of Commons
OTTAWA
Ontario

August 22nd 1984

Dear Mr. Broadbent,

     I have to confess that I almost voted NDP on one or
two occasions in the past, but at the last moment opted in favour
of the Liberals. Sorry!

     However, with the election next month, I have been closely
monitoring the various merits of the campaigning parties, and frankly
this time the Liberals are unlikely to sustain my support.

     John Turner would appear to be a bland, apathetic sort,
with a disgraceful reticence - not a patch on his predecessor.

     I considered Mulroney briefly, but he appears blessed
with qualities more suited to a vacuum cleaner salesman than the
leader of a major political party. Britain voted Conservative,
the result of which was a deflated currency, and inflated unemployment,
the last inflictions Canada needs at the moment.

     So Mr. Broadbent, assuming that you are able to satisfy
my one major misgiving regarding your party manifesto, I and my
colleagues will back you to the hilt.

     I refer of course to your promise to establish full
equality for women. Naturally I applaud any move toward democracy
in the real sense, but we in the Medical profession are becoming
increasingly concerned that the effects of vociferous minority
groups attempting to persuade women that they are identical to men
in all mental and physical abilities, is having a seriously disturbing
affect on the fair sex. All too often nowadays, I see more and more
female patients with personal problems as a direct result of pressure
to be 'equals'.

     Women are gullible creatures, bless them, and to assault
them from all sides with propaganda encouraging them to quash their
valuable natural instincts in favour of pursuits dictated by headline
seeking minorities, is frankly less than sporting.

......./2

I appreciate your party will greatly benefit by courting the large and undecided female vote - nothing wrong with that - but I feel strongly that it is unfair to offer an incentive that few women need or want.

The canvassing of blacks, homosexuals and women at election time in order to temporarily boost ones popularity, is usually the last resort of a party of little substance, and I would not care to think that my vote would be cast to anyone subscribing to such tactics.

Assuming therefore that you are able to assure me that this equality business is not to be taken too seriously, you may be assured of new support for the NDP in this election.

I look forward to your early reassurances.

Yours sincerely,

Bruce West

OFFICE OF THE LEADER
NEW DEMOCRATIC PARTY

BUREAU DU CHEF
NOUVEAU PARTI DÉMOCRATIQUE

DEC 20 1984

Mr. Bruce West
309-941 West 13th Avenue
Vancouver, B.C.
V5Z 1P4

Dear Mr. West:

   Please accept my sincere apologies for the delay
in responding to your letter.

Canadian women are confronted by inequality in all aspects
of their lives. The New Democratic Party believes
that equality between the sexes is fundamental in a
democratic society. In advocating full social and
economic equality between men and women, we are not
arguing that men and women are identical.

   Again, please accept my apologies for the delay
in responding to your letter.

                              Yours sincerely,

P.S. — Merry Christmas!

309-941 West 13th Avenue
Vancouver
British Columbia
V5Z 1P4

Canadian Conference of Catholic Bishops
90 Parent Avenue
Ottawa
Ontario K1N 7B1

October 22nd 1984

For the attention of Most Reverend John Sherlock

Dear Most Reverend Father,

My conscience directs my hand to beg your guidance over a deeply distressing incident which has been my recent experience.

I was proceeding about my lawful occasion down a main street late one evening, when my attention was engaged by a young lady whose attire was startling to say the least, particularly in view of the cold weather. She seemed friendly enough however, and being new to this country I was pleased to stop for a chat.

Then to my horror, it suddenly dawned on me that I was being propositioned by a lady of questionable morals, and panic stricken, I fled without further ado.

My lord, did I act correctly? Was it right to have forsaken the wretched Jezebel without taking corrective action? On reflection perhaps I should have invited her to my modest garret and instructed her as to the error of her sinful ways. Or should I have assumed the more severe alternative and summoned a constable to despatch her to the cells for a sound flogging by the duty officer?

I am unfamiliar with the modern ways of the people of this country, and unsure as to the permitted code of behaviour.

Should a repetition of an incident of this type befall me in the future, what is the course of action which should be adopted?

I await your wise counsel, and apologise for troubling you over this distasteful incident.

Yours sincerely,

Bruce West

Copies to: John Crosbie, Attorney General.
          Commander R. H. Simmonds, R.C.M.P.

Canadian Conference of Catholic Bishops
Conférence des évêques catholiques du Canada

November 5, 1984

Mr. Bruce West
309-941 West 13th Avenue
Vancouver, B.C.
V5Z 1P4

Dear Mr. West:

      Bishop John Sherlock, the President of the CCCB, shared your confidential letter with me and asked me to answer on his behalf.

      From your letter, I would surmise you would wish to have more than a short answer - and an answer which could respect the seriousness and delicacy evident in your question.

      For this reason, I would suggest that you consider contacting a priest in Vancouver and discuss your questions fully with him. I hope that this will provide the assistance which you seek.

      Trusting this is of help.

      Sincerely,

      (Msgr.) Dennis J. Murphy
        General Secretary

90, Parent Avenue, Ottawa, Canada, K1N 7B1 (613) 236-9461 Telex 053-3311

309-941 West 13th Avenue
Vancouver
British Columbia
V5Z 1P4

House of Commons
OTTAWA
Ontario
K1A 0A6

October 22nd 1984

For the attention of John Crosbie
Minister of Justice & Attorney General

Dear Crosbie,

        Enclosed is a copy of my letter to Most Reverend
John Sherlock, the shocking contents of which I know you will
agree are an outrage upon decency.

        For God's sake man, what do you intend to do about
it? Is it too much to expect our streets to be safe for a
Christian gentleman to pass unmolested by fallen women of
this stripe?

        Before coming to this country I was lead by your
government to believe that your nation comprised civilised
people with a fine sense of decency and moral character.
The reality is evidently the very antithesis of all these claims.

        I demand Sir, that you introduce immediate legislation
to remedy this epidemic of moral anarchy.

                              Yours sincerely,

                              Bruce West

Enc.

309-941 West 13th Avenue
Vancouver
British Columbia
V5Z 1P4

House of Commons
OTTAWA
Ontario
K1A 0A6

December 17th 1984

For the attention of John Crosbie
Minister of Justice & Attorney General

Dear Mr. Crosbie,

I wrote to you on October 22nd over a matter of grave moral consequence, and to date I have heard nothing from you regarding this serious issue.

Is your Department also afflicted by the epidemic of moral anarchy discussed in my letter?

With great sadness, I enclose a dollar to facilitate your reply to my questions. No doubt you will let me know if this is insufficient to cover your expenses in performing the obligations of your Office?

Yours sincerely,

Bruce West

Enc.

■✦■ Cabinet du Ministre de la Justice   Office of the Minister of Justice
     et Procureur général du Canada   and Attorney General of Canada

     Ottawa, Canada
     K1A 0H8

January 23, 1985

Mr. Bruce West
309 - 941 West 13th Avenue
Vancouver, British Columbia
V5Z 1P4

Dear Mr. West:

The Honourable John C. Crosbie, Minister of Justice and
Attorney General of Canada, has asked me to reply to your two
recent letters concerning street soliciting. The Minister is
aware that several major cities are experiencing real
problems stemming from an increase in street soliciting for
the purpose of prostitution.

Although in 1983 the Standing Committee on Justice and Legal
Affairs put forth recommendations for legislative action, the
previous government decided to appoint a committee to inquire
into all aspects of the problem in order to determine the
most effective solutions.

You will be interested to know that the Special Committee on
Pornography and Prostitution is presently preparing a report
of its findings. The Committee has benefited from sub-
missions and briefs received in the public hearings and from
information received from a program of empirical research
recently completed by the Department of Justice.

I can assure you that Mr. Crosbie considers legislative
measures to deal with this situation to be a priority. I am
herewith returning your cheque.

Yours sincerely,

James A. Good
Chief of Staff

Enclosure

Canada

309-941 West 13th Avenue
Vancouver
British Columbia
V5Z 1P4

McMillan Binch
Box 38
Royal Bank Plaza
Toronto
Ontario
M5J 2J7

October 28th 1984

For the attention of W. A. Macdonald Q.C.

Dear Mr. Macdonald,

        Your name has been highly recommended to me as a legal
practitioner with the expertise necessary to accommodate an
acquaintance of mine who has been unwise enough to attract the
attentions of the Royal Canadian Mounted Police over a narcotics
incident.

        My friend has not contacted you personally in these
exploratory stages (although he lives rather closer to you than I)
as he wishes to remain anonymous for personal reasons until we
ascertain your interest in handling a case of this nature.

        Perhaps you could indicate your availability and likely
fee structure to expedite this matter at your earliest?

        I understand your firm used to employ John Turner, the
ex-Prime Minister. I'm not a Liberal myself, but I assume politics
don't enter into your procedure for client selection?

        I look forward to your good advices.

                                Yours sincerely,

                                Bruce West

McMILLAN, BINCH

BARRISTERS & SOLICITORS

P.O. BOX 38
SOUTH TOWER
ROYAL BANK PLAZA
TORONTO, ONTARIO
M5J 2J7

TELEPHONE (416) 865-7111
TELEX NO. 06-22317
CABLE ADDRESS "WARDRITE"
TELECOPIER NO. (416) 865-7048

W. A. MACDONALD, Q.C.
DIRECT LINE 865-7091

October 31st, 1984.

Bruce West, Esquire,
309-941 West 13th Avenue,
Vancouver,
British Columbia,
V5Z 1P4.

Dear Mr. West:

Thank you for your letter of October 28th. I don't know who recommended me as a legal practitioner with the kind of expertise you describe. In fact, I have no such expertise and our firm does not handle potential criminal matters other than those relating to combines.

I am sorry that we cannot accommodate your friend but he should have no difficulty in obtaining able counsel to advise him.

Yours very truly,

W. A. Macdonald.

309-941 West 13th Avenue
Vancouver
British Columbia
V5Z 1P4

McMillan Binch
P.O.Box 38
South Tower
Royal Bank Plaza   November 6th 1984
Toronto
Ontario
M5J 2J7

For the attention of W. A. Macdonald Q.C.

Dear Mr. Macdonald,

        Thank you for your astonishing letter dated October 31st,
wherein you state that you specialise in crimes committed by
agricultural apparatus!

        I find it difficult to believe that offences perpetrated
by reaping and threshing machinery in downtown Toronto are
sufficiently prolific to be deserving of your litigious attentions?

        I expect you know what you are doing.

        However, I shall take your kind advice and seek a more
broadly qualified practitioner with the pertinent experience
necessary to assist my compatriot.

                                      Yours sincerely,

                                      Bruce West

309-941 West 13th Avenue
Vancouver
British Columbia
Canada V5Z 1P4

Elite Model Management Corp.
150 E. 58th Avenue
New York
N.Y. 10155
U.S.A.

November 20th 1984

For the attention of John Casablancas

Dear John,

      It is my pleasant responsibility to be charged with
organising my Rowing Club Old Boys annual get-together on
Friday December 21st at a top downtown Toronto hotel.

      There will be fifteen of us in all, and to complete
the occasion we need an equal number of 'models' for the
evening. The girls will be flown to the hotel at our expense
on the Friday afternoon, and returned the following morning,
again all expenses covered.

      We are all wealthy businessmen, so money is no obstacle,
and I need hardly mention the girls will also be well catered
for in the food and drink department!

      Perhaps you could initially send details and photographs
of a selection of your best types, together with an indication
of the total cost, and I will send a cheque by return of post.

      I look forward to doing business with you.

Yours sincerely,

Bruce West

309-941 West 13th Avenue
Vancouver
British Columbia
Canada V5Z 1P4

Elite Model Management Corp.
150 E. 58th Avenue
New York
N.Y. 10155
U.S.A.

December 10th 1984

For the attention of John Casablancas

Dear John,

      Further to my letter of November 20th, our Rowing Club
Old Boys annual dinner has had to be postponed until Saturday
February 2nd next year, as we were unable to secure accommodation
in an hotel appropriate to the status of the occasion on the
proposed date of December 21st.

      The downtown Toronto location has not changed however,
and I trust this new date will be satisfactory to your girls?

      I enclose a deposit of two dollars, and look forward to
receiving details of our order by return post.

      Many thanks in anticipation.

Yours sincerely,

Bruce West

Enc.

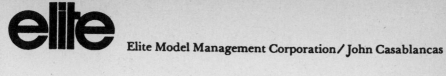

January 3, 1985

Mr. Bruce West
309-941 West 13th Avenue
Vancouver
British Columbia
Canada V5Z 1P4

Dear Mr. West:

Please find enclosed your check dated December 12th in the amount of $2.00.

Unfortunately, Elite will not be able to participate in your annual dinner promotion, and I am therefore returning your check.

Very truly yours,

Loretta Wojcik
Secretary to Mr. Casablancas

JC/lw

enc.

150 East 58th Street • New York, N.Y. 10155 • Tel. (212) 888-6299 • Telex: INYL-428546 • DES 64-9422

309-941 West 13th Avenue
Vancouver
British Columbia
V5Z 1P4

T. Eaton Co. Ltd
1 Dundas Street West
Toronto
Ontario   November 30th 1984
M5B 1C8

For the attention of F. S. Eaton
Chairman

Dear Mr. Eaton,

        This is indeed a sad day for democracy, as picket lines
are set up to reinforce the strike by ungrateful workers at your
excellent Stores.

        Happily I am able to report that you are not alone in
your struggle to keep the employee in his proper place - my own
companies have recently emerged victorious from a revolt within
the ranks, which we were able to quell with methods which would
nowadays be subject to unfavourable review by the Media.

        To this end, I am putting my people in Toronto at your
disposal, and as soon as I give the word they will swoop from
nowhere and pass among the striking rabble with stout clubs and
like deterrents, and having despatched the assembly will quickly
disappear again as if by magic!

        Which areas do you wish attended first? Shall we concentrate
on Metro Toronto, or take in all the picketed Stores?

        As a start I enclose five dollars. Use it as down payment
on a Water Cannon to irrigate the pickets!

        I await your immediate instructions.

                                    Yours sincerely,

                                    Bruce West

Enc.

EATON'S

Office of the President

Toronto Canada M5B 1C8

F.S. Eaton	President, Chairman and Chief Executive Officer
G.R. Eaton	Executive Vice President and Deputy Chairman
G.R. Purchase	Executive Vice President and Chief Operating Officer

December 10, 1984

Bruce West Esq.,
941 W. 13th Avenue,
Apartment #309
Vancouver.   British Columbia
V5Z 1P4

Dear Mr. West:

Thank you for your supportive letter and the
cheque you enclosed.   It was very thoughtful
of you, but I am returning your cheque because
while I appreciate very much your gesture, I
think we can win this one on our own, and would
prefer you either keep your money or donate it
to some worthy cause such as the United Way.

It is good to see that we have so many friends
across Canada, from whom we have been receiving
solid support.   For your interest I am attaching
a copy of a letter sent to All Bargaining Unit
Employees.

Again, thank you for writing and may I take this
opportunity of sending my very best wishes for
the Holiday Season.

Yours) sincerely,

Fredrik S. Eaton

309-941 West 13th Avenue
Vancouver
British Columbia
Canada V5Z 1P4

Ayatollah Ruhollah Khomeini
State Offices
Tehran
<u>IRAN</u>

January 4th 1986

Your Excellency,

        I imagine by now you must be thoroughly fed up with
reading about and listening to short-sighted criticism of
your monotheistic dictatorship since the departure of the
late Shah of Iran?

        When I was attending College some years back, it was
my privilege to study with a considerable number of students
from Iran, and if I may say so, I always found them to be
most pugilistic and unsavoury in every regard!

        In my humble opinion therefore, I cannot agree with
world condemnation of the wholesale execution of those found
guilty of serious crime in your fair country, as I have yet
to meet one of your fellow countrymen undeserving of suitable
peremptory correction!

        On the contrary, a simple people such as yours benefits
from and indeed needs sound leadership from a lucid and
compassionate ruler of your eminence!

        May I therefore extend a warm hand of international
friendship to you in your hours of turbulence, and request
a signed photo of Your Excellency in your splendid Official
Regalia to take pride of place in my modest gallery of
benevolent Conservatives?

                        Yours respectfully,

                        Bruce West

309-941 West 13th Avenue
Vancouver
British Columbia
Canada V5Z 1P4

Ayatollah Ruhollah Khomeini
State Offices
Tehran
IRAN   February 19th 1986

Your Excellency,

        What's the post like in your neck of the woods?

        My humble request of January 4th for a photograph
of your Highness to adorn my Gallery of Great Statesmen
has yet to bear fruit!

        One assumes that you keep a few snaps handy to
amuse your few admirers - of course I could always pop
over personally with my Kodak but I expect you are far
too busy with internal executions and the like to pose
for me!

        I enclose two dollars to pay for your development
costs, and look forward to receiving my photograph in early
course!

        God bless you!

                        Yours in Admiration,

                        Bruce West

Enc.

Bruce West
309-941 west 13th Ave
Vancouver British
Columbia Canada
V5Z - 1P4

BY AIR MAIL
PAR AVION

309-941 West 13th Avenue
Vancouver
British Columbia
V5Z 1P4

Molson Ontario Breweries Ltd
640 Fleet Street West
Toronto
Ontario   December 22nd 1984
M5V 1B2

For the attention of D. A. Barbour
President

Dear Mr. Barbour,

        My new restaurant opens its doors for business at the
beginning of February next year, and I have therefore been obliged
to sample the various beers available on the market in order to
decide which brands to stock.

        I think I can safely claim to have a discerning palate,
and I am disappointed to report that they all taste the same to
me, bland, characterless, and uncomfortably gaseous. However, in
spite of the lack of positive incentive from any of the varieties
sampled, I have decided to stock Molson, on the assumption that
your advertising is probably best geared to induce the mugs to
resort to your particular beverages.

        It has always seemed to me to be an unfortunate irony
that social and legislative pressure dictates that alcoholic
drink advertising obliges breweries to concoct subtle scenes of
pleasant sporting activities, up-market social gatherings, and
similar views of pretty women and well-off men, when probably one
would be making a far more accurate and effective advert by coming
straight to the point with, for instance, "O.K. guys, so it tastes
as though it's been re-cycled through an Algerian donkey a couple
of times, but if you drink it cold enough you can't taste it anyway,
and at least you can get pissed on it which is what it's all about!"

        Ah well, such is life.

        I should incidentally like to extend an invitation to you
to attend the opening of the Restaurant next February, and perhaps
even to make a small speech to the assembled Press and local
Dignitarys. Perhaps you might pencil this in your diary, and I
will contact you with further details next month?

                              Yours sincerely,

                              Bruce West

MOLSON

OFFICE OF THE PRESIDENT

January 4, 1985.

Mr. Bruce West,
309 - 941 West 13th Avenue,
Vancouver, B.C.
V5Z 1P4

Dear Mr. West:

Thank you for your letter. I have referred it to Mr. Jack Beach,
President, Molson Brewery B.C. Ltd.

I am somewhat puzzled by your remarks about beer in general as well
as your suggested advertising copy. Surely you cannot be serious!

I trust that, if you decide to sell our products, we will have some
assurances that they will be presented in a positive manner to your
customers. Canadian beer, and Molson brands in particular, are of
the finest in the world. We would not want them represented in any
other way.

Yours sincerely,

David A. Barbour
President

cc. N. M. Seagram
     J. G. Beach

MOLSON ONTARIO BREWERIES LIMITED
640 Fleet Street, Toronto, Ontario M5V 1B2, Tel. (416) 869-1786, Telex 06218289

309-941 West 13th Avenue
Vancouver
British Columbia
V5Z 1P4

Canadian Broadcasting Corporation
1500 Bronson Avenue
P.O.Box 8478
Ottawa
Ontario K1G 3J5

November 12th 1984

For the attention of Pierre Juneau
<u>President</u>

Dear Mr. Juneau,

I was concerned to learn that Government cut-backs are
being applied to the CBC's budget, and I trust this will not
result in television programming becoming even worse than it is
now?

To compensate for the reduced finances, I have one or
two suggestions which you may care to consider.

1. Shake off the dowdy image projected by your News
Readers - reporters like Barbara Frum are more than able to read
the News, but it's glamour that sells the product. Rope in a
few young starlets wearing revealing low-cut dresses. If their
enunciation is not quite up to par, no-one will notice!

11. Scrap documentaries and other so-called serious
programmes, no-one watches them anyway. Pornography and
gratuitous violence is where it's at nowadays, as any reputable
video shop proprietor will confirm.

111. Try to employ programme co-ordinators who know
how to cut-in the Commercials without chopping off both ends of
the Advert! This will please the advertisers, and the viewers
might be able to discover the identity of the product they are
being bamboozled into buying!

Here's a dollar. Not much, but if every responsible
viewer took his National Broadcasting as seriously as this
writer, funds would soon mount up.

Yours sincerely,

Bruce West

Enc.

Canadian   Société
Broadcasting   Radio-
Corporation   Canada

P.O. Box 8478
Ottawa, Ontario
K1G 3J5

December 13, 1984

Mr. Bruce West
309 - 941 West 13th Avenue
Vancouver, B.C.
V5Z 1P4

Dear Mr. West:

Thank you for your letter of November
12, which arrived in this office
December 10.

Note has been taken of your three
programming suggestions, and your
cheque for one dollar, made out in
the name of Pierre Juneau, is enclosed
herewith.

Yours sincerely,

Eleanor Strayer
Special Assistant
  to the President.

309-941 West 13th Avenue
Vancouver
British Columbia
V5Z 1P4

Canadian Broadcasting Corporation
P.O.Box 8478
Ottawa
Ontario
K1G 3J5

December 19th 1984

For the attention of Eleanor Strayer
<u>Special Assistant to the President</u>

Dear Eleanor,

     Thank you for your rather mystifying letter of December 13th, returning my cheque for one dollar.

     It would appear that things at the CBC are not quite as bad as we are lead to believe, as not only can you manage without my donation, but you can also afford to return it via Registered Mail at a cost to yourselves of $2.28!

     I'm sure you know best.

Yours sincerely,

Bruce West

309-941 West 13th Avenue
Vancouver
British Columbia
V5Z 1P4

Heenan, Blaikie, Jolin,
Potvin, Trepanier, Cobbett.
1400-1001, De Maisonneuve Blvd. W.
Montreal
Quebec H3A 3C8

November 8th 1984

For the attention of Pierre Trudeau

Dear Mr. Trudeau,

    Forgive me for writing from my 'out of town' address, I am
here to settle some pressing business matters for a week or two.

    My latest book is almost ready for delivery to my publisher,
and in view of its uniquely perspicacious insight into the very
heart of the most fascinating aspects of political and corporate
activity, subjects in which you have immense experience and
expertise, I would be honoured if you would consider writing
the Foreword.

    A substantial fee, or generous share of the royalties would
be a minor consideration for the privilege of a short delivery
from the pen of a man who, may I say, has always to me been the
quintessential Statesman, considerably understated by your recently
retired appellation.

    Naturally you will want to savour the rich and stimulating
text before committing yourself, and to that end I am having a
proof prepared for your early scrutiny.

    I shall be in Montreal on Monday, November 26th, and will
drop in to present the manuscript for your comments at about 12.30,
unless I hear from you that an alternative time would be more
convenient.

    I look forward to meeting you.

Yours sincerely,

Bruce West

309-941 West 13th Avenue
Vancouver
British Columbia
V5Z 1P4

Canadian Broadcasting Corporation
1500 Bronson Avenue
P.O.Box 8478
Ottawa   November 12th 1984
Ontario K1G 3J5

For the attention of Pierre Juneau
<u>President</u>

Dear Mr. Juneau,

        I was concerned to learn that Government cut-backs are
being applied to the CBC's budget, and I trust this will not
result in television programming becoming even worse than it is
now?

        To compensate for the reduced finances, I have one or
two suggestions which you may care to consider.

        1. Shake off the dowdy image projected by your News
Readers - reporters like Barbara Frum are more than able to read
the News, but it's glamour that sells the product. Rope in a
few young starlets wearing revealing low-cut dresses. If their
enunciation is not quite up to par, no-one will notice!

        11. Scrap documentaries and other so-called serious
programmes, no-one watches them anyway. Pornography and
gratuitous violence is where it's at nowadays, as any reputable
video shop proprietor will confirm.

        111. Try to employ programme co-ordinators who know
how to cut-in the Commercials without chopping off both ends of
the Advert! This will please the advertisers, and the viewers
might be able to discover the identity of the product they are
being bamboozled into buying!

        Here's a dollar. Not much, but if every responsible
viewer took his National Broadcasting as seriously as this
writer, funds would soon mount up.

                              Yours sincerely,

                              Bruce West

Enc.

Canadian   Société
Broadcasting   Radio-
Corporation   Canada

P.O. Box 8478
Ottawa, Ontario
K1G 3J5

December 13, 1984

Mr. Bruce West
309 - 941 West 13th Avenue
Vancouver, B.C.
V5Z 1P4

Dear Mr. West:

Thank you for your letter of November
12, which arrived in this office
December 10.

Note has been taken of your three
programming suggestions, and your
cheque for one dollar, made out in
the name of Pierre Juneau, is enclosed
herewith.

Yours sincerely,

Eleanor Strayer
Special Assistant
    to the President.

309-941 West 13th Avenue
Vancouver
British Columbia
V5Z 1P4

Canadian Broadcasting Corporation
P.O.Box 8478
Ottawa
Ontario
K1G 3J5

December 19th 1984

For the attention of Eleanor Strayer
Special Assistant to the President

Dear Eleanor,

Thank you for your rather mystifying letter of
December 13th, returning my cheque for one dollar.

It would appear that things at the CBC are not
quite as bad as we are lead to believe, as not only can you
manage without my donation, but you can also afford to return
it via Registered Mail at a cost to yourselves of $2.28!

I'm sure you know best.

Yours sincerely,

Bruce West

309-941 West 13th Avenue
Vancouver
British Columbia
V5Z 1P4

Heenan, Blaikie, Jolin,
Potvin, Trepanier, Cobbett.
1400-1001, De Maisonneuve Blvd. W.
Montreal
Quebec H3A 3C8

November 8th 1984

<u>For the attention of Pierre Trudeau</u>

Dear Mr. Trudeau,

Forgive me for writing from my 'out of town' address, I am
here to settle some pressing business matters for a week or two.

My latest book is almost ready for delivery to my publisher,
and in view of its uniquely perspicacious insight into the very
heart of the most fascinating aspects of political and corporate
activity, subjects in which you have immense experience and
expertise, I would be honoured if you would consider writing
the Foreword.

A substantial fee, or generous share of the royalties would
be a minor consideration for the privilege of a short delivery
from the pen of a man who, may I say, has always to me been the
quintessential Statesman, considerably understated by your recently
retired appellation.

Naturally you will want to savour the rich and stimulating
text before committing yourself, and to that end I am having a
proof prepared for your early scrutiny.

I shall be in Montreal on Monday, November 26th, and will
drop in to present the manuscript for your comments at about 12.30,
unless I hear from you that an alternative time would be more
convenient.

I look forward to meeting you.

Yours sincerely,

Bruce West

Pierre Elliott Trudeau

1001 BOUL. DE MAISONNEUVE OUEST
SUITE 1400
MONTRÉAL, QUÉBEC H3A 3C8
(514) 281-1212

November 20, 1984

Mr. Bruce West
309-941 West 13th Avenue
Vancouver, British Columbia
V5Z 1P4

Dear Sir:

      I acknowledge receipt of your letter of
November 8, regarding the book you have written
and asking me if I would consider writing the
Foreword.

      In reply, I must inform you that since
my retirement from active political life, I have
been enjoying a «sabbatical» and therefore
endeavouring to keep a low profile. For this
reason, I do not feel that I can accept your
invitation at this time.

      I regret that I am unable to give you a
more favourable reply, but rest assured of my very
best wishes for the success of your book.

                Sincerely,

                Pierre Elliott Trudeau

PET:gb

309-941 West 13th Avenue
Vancouver
British Columbia
V5Z 1P4

Heenan, Blaikie, Jolin,
Potvin, Trepanier, Cobbett.
1400-1001, De Maisonneuve Blvd. W.
Montreal
Quebec H3A 3C8

November 23rd 1984

For the attention of Pierre Trudeau

Dear Mr. Trudeau,

        Thank you for your letter of November 20th, and I am
naturally disappointed that you are unable to commit yourself
to writing the Foreword to my book.

        The work will, in my humble opinion, be favourably
received by the upper echelons of critics of corporate and
political function, and your prevalent image might well have
enjoyed the refreshing benefit of an approbatory Press, through
your personal endorsement of the Text.

        I respect your wishes however, and fully understand
that having been responsible for leading the Country and the
Liberal Party for so many years, you are obliged to lie low
for a while!

        May I take this opportunity to wish you a peaceful
and well deserved retirement from your former activities.

                        Yours sincerely,

                        Bruce West

309-941 West 13th Avenue
Vancouver
British Columbia
V5Z 1P4

Harlequin Enterprises Ltd
225 Duncan Mill Road
Don Mills
Ontario
M3B 1Z3

May 15th 1985

For the attention of Brian Hickey
<u>President North America</u>

Dear Brian,

      I am presently completing my latest work, a book of
unusual consequence which is a unique diversification from
the type of narrative to which my reputation is usually
attributed.

      I am convinced that the content of this collection
will appeal to the taste of the reader for whom your good
House caters, and thus offer you first option to publish,
subject to my usual terms and stipulations.

      Briefly, the book encompasses a tantalising variety
of plot, including amongst others the gripping subjects of
assassination, foreign travel, drugs, pop stars, Royalty,
top level litigation, police corruption, bizarre religious
cults, The Armed Forces, The Mounties, prostitution, mail
robbery, celebrity banquets, show business, poisoning,
multi-million dollar bank deals, company takeovers, murder
abroad, corporal punishment, political corruption, imminent
World War, women's issues, senior governmental incompetence,
high finance, religion, sex, torture and parliamentary scandal!

      I know you will be eager to confirm your interest in
securing the publishing rights without delay, and look forward
to receiving a substantial advance and your proposals by return
post.

      I enclose two dollars to cover your expenses in this
matter.

Yours sincerely,

Bruce West

Enc.

RICHARD H. CHENOWETH
DIRECTOR
VENTURES GROUP

Harlequin Books

225 Duncan Mill Road, Don Mills, Ontario, Canada M3B 3K9

(416) 445-5860   Telex 06-966697

June 12, 1985

Mr. Bruce West
309 - 941 West 13th Avenue
Vancouver, B.C.
V5Z 1P4

Dear Mr. West:

Brian Hickey has asked me to respond to your letter of May 15, 1985 regarding your latest work.

Several aspects of your proposal create problems for me:

. I personally am not familiar with... "The type of narrative to which your reputation is usually attributed."

. Again, I am not familiar with your "usual terms and stipulations" under which you grant publishing rights.

. Your description of the work is too generalized and inadequate to evaluate the work. In an instance such as this, we only would consider negotiating for publishing rights upon our review of the completed manuscript.

As a result of these problems, I cannot confirm our interest in your work and will not be forwarding a "substantial advance" or a proposal. I do enclose your uncashed cheque for $2.00 submitted by you to cover our expenses in this matter.

Yours truly,

R.H. Chenoweth
Director Ventures Group

RHC:zw

Encl.

309-941 West 13th Avenue
Vancouver
British Columbia
V5Z 1P4

Canada Post Corporation
Confederation Heights
Ottawa
Ontario
K1A 0B1

October 22nd 1984

For the attention of Michael Warren
<u>President</u>

Dear Mr. Warren,

You can imagine my surprise this morning, when I switched on the radio to hear the news of a possible strike by postal workers.

Those of us in the business community were completely unaware that your Corporation was not already on strike!

If the radio report is accurate and your employees have not yet ceased to function and they do strike, what possible reduction in postal service could be the result?

A quick survey of my executives indicates conclusively that the only avenue left open to further deteriorate productivity would be for you to despatch armed operatives to take back the mail already delivered!

This course of action would not cause too much inconvenience to us incidentally, as by the time the mail arrives it is usually too old to be of value anyway.

I am posting this letter at precisely midday today, and await with interest the date I receive your reply, which will serve as a visible measurement of the efficiency of the postal operation.

Yours sincerely,

Bruce West

Canada Post
Corporation

Société canadienne
des postes

Office of the
President and Chief
Executive Officer

Cabinet du
Président –
directeur général

Ottawa, Canada
K1A 0B1

November 5, 1984

Mr. Bruce West
309 - 941 West 13th Avenue
VANCOUVER, B.C.
V5Z 1P4

Dear Mr. West:

     I am writing to acknowledge receipt of your letter of October 22
to Mr. R. Michael Warren, President of the Canada Post Corporation,
commenting on the postal service.

     Please be assured that your comments have been brought to
Mr. Warren's attention.

                          Yours sincerely,

                          Esther Christopher
                          Manager
                          Correspondence Unit

Canada

309-941 West 13th Avenue
Vancouver
British Columbia
V5Z 1P4

Canada Post Corporation
Ottawa
Ontario
K1A OB1

November 8th 1984

For the attention of Michael Warren
<u>President</u>

Dear Warren,

Please thank your assistant, Esther Christopher for the reply to my letter of October 22nd, which I received this morning.

Why can't you answer your own correspondence?

I went to the trouble of writing to you personally, why should I not be afforded the reciprocal courtesy?

If I have occasion to communicate with you again, I shall address you through my chauffeur.

Yours sincerely,

Bruce West

309-941 West 13th Avenue
Vancouver
British Columbia
V5Z 1P4

Department of National Defence
101 Colonel By Drive
Ottawa
Ontario   October 23rd 1984
K1A 0K2

For the attention of Brigadier-General J. Y. Durocher C.D.

Dear Brigadier-General,

        I am very interested in a career in the Armed Forces,
and gather that you are the fellow to advise in these matters.

        Where does one start?

        To be honest, the Air Force might not be up my street,
as I'm inclined to be slightly acrophobic.

        What about the Navy? Sounds pretty exciting, and I've
always liked the sea, but I'm a bit put off by the disparaging
remarks in the Press concerning the apparently decrepit condition
of our ships. If what one reads is true the Fleet can barely
sail out of its' own harbour without succumbing to involuntary
submarine duty!

        On balance I think the Army might be the best bet. I
don't have much experience at violence and killing, but I'm
willing to learn.

        What in your opinion are the chances of getting shot?
I'm looking for a long term career, and should be keen to know
the current statistics in this area.

        Are promotions awarded on a frequent basis? How long
would it take for example to attain the rank of Brigadier-
General like yourself?

        I look forward eagerly to your reply and suggestions.

                                        Yours sincerely,

                                        Bruce West

National Defence   Défense nationale

National Defence Headquarters   Quartier général de la Défense nationale
Ottawa, Canada   Ottawa, Canada
K1A 0K2   K1A 0K2

1351-500/W (DG Info)

29 October, 1984

Bruce West
309 - 941 West 13th Avenue
Vancouver, B.C.
V5Z 1P4

Dear Bruce West:

       Thank you for your letter of 23 October, 1984
in which you requested information on careers in the
Canadian Forces.

       I must inform you at the very outset that in
1964, Parliament authorized the Department of National
Defence to integrate the three services of the Armed
Forces. On 1 February, 1968, the Canadian Forces
Reorganization Act was passed and the Royal Canadian
Navy, the Canadian Army and the Royal Canadian Air Force
ceased to exist as legal entities.

       Combining the three services was accomplished
in two phases. The first phase, integration, involved
the creation and implementation of orders and regulations
to permit the grouping of the three services under one
command structure or headquarters, supported by integrated
logistics and training systems. The three services still
retained their separate identities under the new command
structure.

       The second phase, unification, saw the creation
of a single service. All members were issued a common
uniform and administered under one personnel policy.

                                            .../2

Canada

For information about careers in the Canadian
Forces, admission requirements, Officer entry plans,
Other Ranks entry plans, length of service, dress
regulations, pay and benefits and training, please visit
our Canadian Forces Recruiting Centre in your locality.
For your convenience, the address is:

        Canadian Forces Recruiting Centre
        547 Seymour Street
        Vancouver, B.C.
        V6B 3H6

        Telephone: (604) 666-3136

        I thank you for your interest in the Canadian
Forces, and hope that the information provided will
assist you in your choice of a career in the Canadian
Forces.

                                Yours sincerely,

                                J.Y. Durocher
                                Brigadier-General
                                Director General Information

309-941 West 13th Avenue
Vancouver
British Columbia
V5Z 1P4

The Toronto Stock Exchange
2 First Canadian Place
Toronto
Ontario
M5X 1J2

November 23rd 1984

For the attention of J. Pearce Bunting
President

Dear Mr. Bunting,

        In light of a couple of close shaves with the Constabulary
in recent months, I am obliged to retire from my usual 'business'
for a while, and dispose of the proceeds before we are forcibly
separated!

        I am reliably informed that the Stock Market is not a
bad number to get into if you know your way around, and I gather
one can rely on absolute discretion regarding the origin of the
funds your people accept for investment?

        I have a considerable amount (in cash!) to lay out as
quickly as possible, and as soon as you let me know the score,
I will hot-foot to your Office with the necessary in hand.

        Needless to say, if you can get me pointed in the right
direction with no unnecessary fuss, there will be 'something in it'
for you personally.

        I look forward to your early advice.

                              Yours sincerely,

                              Bruce West

The Exchange

The Exchange Tower
2 First Canadian Place
Toronto, Canada M5X 1J2
(416) 947-4700

December 18, 1984

Mr. Bruce West
309-941 West 13th Avenue
Vancouver, B.C.
V5Z 1P4

Dear Mr. West:

Further to your recent letter with regard to investing on the stock market, I have enclosed some general information which you may find useful.

The TSE does not buy or sell stocks on behalf of investors. This means that all business must be transacted through a brokerage firm which is a member of the TSE. In addition you must select a stockbroker from the member firm who will act on your behalf. You will be required to open an account with the brokerage firm before you are permitted to trade. Your stockbroker will advise you on your investment alternatives.

Should you have any further questions, please don't hesitate to contact me.

Yours truly,

Mary M. Revell

Mary M. Revell
Manager,
Information & Media Services

MMR/jc

encls.

                                        309-941 West 13th Avenue
                                        Vancouver
Public Service Commission   British Columbia
P.O. Box 2703   V5Z 1P4
Whitehorse
Yukon Y1A 2C6   December 4th 1984

Dear Sir,

        Regarding the advertised vacancy for Territorial Court
Judge, you need search no further!

        My vast legal expertise has been acquired over a
considerable number of years, and to the eternal frustration
of my opponents thus far I have a spotless record. How many
of us can boast that nowadays?

        You may be assured that all who appear before me for
sentencing will be well advised to prepare themselves for a
long detention, with minimal facilities to ease the passage
of time. Yes Sir, I intend to crack down on trouble makers,
and crack down hard!

        I note the salary for this position is a nominal
$74,345.00 per annum. I would also have to insist on an
aircraft for my personal transportation, and of course a Motor-
Carriage commensurate with the status of the appointment.

        I am not without means, and I am on first name terms
with the Prime Minister.

        I look forward to receiving confirmation of my appointment,
and to expedite same I enclose five dollars to make sure my name
goes straight to the top of the pile.

                                        Yours faithfully,

                                        Bruce West

Enc.

Public Service Commission
Box 2703, Whitehorse, Yukon Y1A 2C6
(403) 667-5811 Telex 036-8-260

Our File:
Your File:

1984 December 11

Mr. Bruce West,
309-941 West 13th Avenue,
Vancouver, B.C.
V5Z 1P4

Dear Mr. West:

I am in receipt of your letter of application dated December 04, 1984 for the position of Territorial Court Judge.

Please be advised that "an aircraft for (my) personal transportation" and "a motor carriage" are not provided with this position.

I am returning your cheque for five dollars ... any attempt to bribe a public official is an offence under the Criminal Code.

Yours sincerely,

Susan L. Priest,
Personnel Officer.

/jp

encl.

Yukon

Public Service Commission
Box 2703, Whitehorse, Yukon Y1A 2C6
(403) 667-5811 Telex 036-8-260

Our File:
Your File:

March 26, 1985

Mr. Bruce West
309-941 West 13th Avenue
Vancouver, B.C.
V5Z 1P4

Dear Mr. West:

Re: Territorial Court Judge
    Competition No. 84-1379-1

I am writing to inform you that, although every consideration has
been given to your application, it was unsuccessful on the above
noted competition.

We invite you to enter future competitions for positions in which you
are interested.

Yours sincerely,

P. Cumming
Director
Recruitment and Labour Relations

/gca

EXPO
86

309-941 West 13th Avenue
Vancouver
British Columbia
V5Z 1P4

House of Commons
OTTAWA
Ontario
K1A 0A6

March 25th 1985

For the attention of Pat Carney
Minister of Energy, Mines & Resources

Dear Mr. Carney,

I represent a consortium of Overseas investors
mainly domiciled in South Africa, who are anxious to get
their assets out of the country before the balloon goes
up, and we are therefore examining the possibility of
commencing a mining operation in Ontario.

My people here have thoroughly researched the
areas we are keen to consider for our venture, and I
should like to meet with you to discuss any Government
tax breaks, subsidies, concessions etc., you could help
us with, plus advice on securing cheap native or immigrant
labour for the operation.

I might mention that our backers are extremely
comfortably heeled, and any 'unofficial' assistance you
may favour us with will not go unrewarded!

I shall be in Ottawa on April 29th, and perhaps
we might meet for luncheon on that date, shall we say
at 12.30?

I look forward greatly to hearing your confirmation
that this time will be suitable, and enclose two dollars to
cover the expense of your reply.

Yours sincerely,

Bruce West

Enc.

APR
AVR 15 1985

Mr. Bruce West
309 - 941 West 13th Avenue
Vancouver, B.C.
V5Z 1P4

Dear Mr. West:

      Thank you for your letter of March 25, 1985,
requesting a meeting with the Honourable Pat Carney,
Minister of Energy, Mines and Resources.

      Unfortunately, due to previous commitments
the Minister will be unable to meet with you as
suggested. Perhaps at a future date, another request
might again be extended.

      I am also returning your cheque for $2.00.

                 Sincerely,

                 Harry Near
                 Chief of Staff

Canadä

309-941 West 13th Avenue
Vancouver
British Columbia
Canada V5Z 1P4

Prime Minister Margaret Thatcher
10 Downing Street
London
S.W.1.
GREAT BRITAIN

July 12th 1985

Dear Prime Minister,

As a loyal British subject, I am writing to express the horror and disgust I felt upon reading a most irreverent report in today's newspaper.

If the article is to be believed, the new British One Pound Coin is now officially referred to as a 'Maggie', on the premise that its' unpopularity is based on it comprising a "Cheap brass bit that thinks it's a Sovereign!"

Apart from my personal condemnation of such cruel numismatic treason, I am also concerned that should Canada also adopt a One Dollar Coin to replace the current paper version, Prime Minister Brian Mulroney might well suffer the same disgraceful allegory to the new currency that you are now enduring.

As you know, Mr. Mulroney is a highly sensitive fellow, by no means a man of the world like yourself, and I know that any below the belt reference to his personal image would wound him terribly.

One anticipates with dread the reaction of the visiting Foreigner proffering a new One Dollar Coin, upon being informed that it was now called a 'Brian', because it was "New to the job, swiftly wore a hole in the pocket, and was thoroughly unconvincing to those unfamiliar with it!"

Any counter-measures you may be able to suggest to shore up Mr. Mulroney's reputation should the new coin be introduced here will be most gratefully received.

With many thanks and warm condolances.

Yours sincerely,

Bruce West

Mr B West
309-941 West 13th Avenue
Vancouver
British Columbia
CANADA
V5Z 1P4

Treasury Chambers
Parliament Street
LONDON
SW1P 3AG
Telex 262405
Telephone Direct Line 01-233
Switchboard 01-233 3000

Our reference
12/7/1
28 August 198

Dear Mr West

£1 COIN

You wrote to the Prime Minister on 12 July concerning an article in a newspaper about the £1 coin. I have been asked to reply and should begin by apologising for the delay in doing so.

As I have not seen the newspaper article to which you refer I cannot, of course, comment. But what I can say is that as far as I am aware, the £1 coin does not have an 'official' title, especially that to which you refer in your letter, over and above being referred to by what it is, namely, a £1 coin. That said, the logic that Prime Minister Brian Mulroney might experience a similar fate is not tenable.

Finally, I return the 2 dollar cheque enclosed with your letter.

Yours sincerely

George Haydon.

G C HAYDON

ENC

PG

309-941 West 13th Avenue
Vancouver
British Columbia
V5Z 1P4

Mr. J.L.Ross, Secretary
Sudbury Regional Board of
Commissioners of Police
69 Young Street
Sudbury
Ontario P3E 3G5

September 9th 1984

Dear Mr. Ross,

In response to your advertisement for a Chief of Police
(Globe & Mail, September 8th), I am pleased to nominate myself for
the position.

Reading between the lines of your advert, I deduce that
you seek a man, like myself, with a background in managing the 'man
in the street' with a firm, yet not overly severe hand.

My actual police experience is limited to a spell as a
Special Constable in the Isle of Man some years back. No matter,
what's needed here is a strong leadership that's not afraid to
start afresh with the stern measures necessary to whip the country
into shape again, undoing the damage inflicted by procrastinating
liberals who have made our streets unsafe for decent folk to walk.

My qualifications have been acquired as a Leader of
Industry, where precisely the sort of authority you seek is vital
to ensure an efficient operation.

That's not to say I don't have some fresh, if perhaps
unconventional ideas on how to crack down on offenders who dare
to step out of line on my Patch.

I shall be in Sudbury on business on Friday, September
28th, and unless I hear to the contrary, I shall drop in to discuss
salary, perks etc., at about 12.30.

Looking forward to meeting you.

Yours sincerely,

Bruce West

SUDBURY
REGIONAL

POLICE

ADDRESS ALL CORRESPONDENCE TO THE SECRETARY

J. L. ROSS
POLICE ADMINISTRATION BUILDING
200 LARCH STREET
SUDBURY, ONTARIO
P3E 1C7   **SUDBURY REGIONAL BOARD OF COMMISSIONERS OF POLICE**

September 14, 1984.

Mr. Bruce West,
309-941 West 13th Avenue,
Vancouver, B. C.
V5Z 1P4

Dear Sir:

RE: Application for position of Chief

This is to acknowledge your letter of September 9th
and to advise it would serve no purpose to attend at Sudbury
September 28th as indicated because no action will be taken on
applications until after the closing date, October 12th.

Yours very truly,

J. L. Ross,
Secretary

309-941 West 13th Avenue
Vancouver
British Columbia
V5Z 1P4

Personnel Officer
Town of Kentville
P.O. Box 218
Kentville
Nova Scotia
B4N 3W4

September 24th 1984

Dear Sir,

Reference the vacancy in the Globe & Mail on September 22nd for a Chief of Police for Kentville, I am pleased to nominate myself for the position.

I note that your Department has a complement of only 13 men, a smaller force than I was hoping for. Nonetheless, I am still willing to consider the position if the other compensations fulfil my expectations.

My own background has encompassed a wide experience of legal procedure, both criminal and civil, and I am happy to confirm that I have never lost a case in either category, as my personal files with the Authorities will testify.

Aside from a short spell some years back as a Special Constable with a small island based foreign power, where the birching of juvenile offenders is still encouraged, my experience on the side of authority is a shade limited.

No matter, my expertise will be a valuable asset to our crime ridden streets, where honest citizens fear to tread, and I would welcome the opportunity to introduce some revolutionary deterrents to rid our long suffering society of the disruptive elements repeatedly set free by doddering liberal judges who are afraid of their own shadows.

I shall be in Nova Scotia on business on Friday October 12th, and unless I hear to the contrary I will drop in at about 12.30 to finalise salary, perks etc.

Looking forward to meeting you.

Yours faithfully,

Bruce West

309-941 West 13th Avenue
Vancouver
British Columbia
V5Z 1P4

Personnel Officer   October 9th 1984
Town of Kentville
P.O.Box 218
Kentville
Nova Scotia
B4N 3W4

Dear Sir,

        I regret that I shall have to postpone our meeting at
your offices on October 12th, per my letter dated September 24th
regarding the position for Chief of Police.

        I was naturally looking forward to inspecting the Men
and concluding the details of my appointment, but I am considering
the contents of an encouraging letter from Mr. J.L.Ross (I expect
you know him) regarding the similar position of Chief at Sudbury,
and thus feel it would be imprudent at this delicate stage of
negotiation to risk raising your hopes, only to disappoint later.

        Should my position alter however, I will be in touch again.

                                        Yours faithfully,

                                        Bruce West

Town of Kentville

DIRECTOR
OF FINANCE

OFFICE OF THE TOWN
CLERK and TREASURER

Telephone (902) 678–2107
354 Main Street,
P.O. Box 218,
Kentville, Nova Scotia
B4N 3W4

Kentville, Nova Scotia

December 4, 1984

Mr. Bruce West,
309-941 West 13th Avenue,
Vancouver, B.C.
V5Z 1P4

Dear Mr. West:

I wish to take this opportunity to express thanks for your interest and application for the position of Chief of Police for the Town of Kentville.

I must advise however, that another individual has been selected for this position. As we received approximately sixty applications the few interviewed were selected on the basis of the information contained in their application.

Once again, thank you for applying and good luck in future endeavors.

Yours truly,

G.D. Morse, CMA,
Director of Finance and Personnel

GDM/sb

309-941 West 13th Avenue
Vancouver
British Columbia
Canada V5Z 1P4

The Coca-Cola Company
310 North Avenue N.W.
Atlanta
Georgia 30313   October 2nd 1984
U.S.A.

For the attention of Roberto C. Goizueta
Chairman

Dear Mr. Goizueta,

        In accord with the majority of responsible physicians
in North America, my colleagues and I are extremely concerned
regarding the alleged toxic properties contained by your dubious
products.

        You will no doubt be aware of the soon to be published
Government Report on 'soft drinks', with particular reference to
the alarmingly coincident deterioration of digestive function now
recognised to be a direct consequence of regular consumption of
beverages of your ilk.

        My own people have been conducting a private research
into the harmful effects suffered by innumerable children and young
adults, drawn to innocent addiction by glamorous advertisements
such as the example currently showing on television, featuring the
quintessentially popular song-and-dance mannequin, Jesse Jackson.

        I submit sir, that the irresponsible employment of pop
stars to foist your wares upon the young and impressionable is a
moral and commercial travesty of monumental proportion.

        Aside from one's professional commitment to this
investigation into the detrimental content of your products, which
have always been widely reputed to have corrosive properties, one's
personal view to this end is compounded by the recent inexplicable
disappearance of a caged hamster belonging to a neighbour's
children, subsequent to their playfully 'rewarding' the unfortunate
rodent with a saucer of Coke.

        You may be assured that my staff will be collaborating
our evidence with the findings of the Authorities, and that our
consequent public disclosures will ensure swift curtailment of
your blatant commercial excesses.

                                        Yours sincerely,

                                        Bruce West

A Division of The Coca-Cola Company

P.O. Drawer 1734, Atlanta, Georgia 30301 404 676-2603

October 24, 1984

Consumer Information Center

Mr. Bruce West
309-941 West 13th Avenue
Vancouver
British Columbia
CANADA V5Z 1P4

Dear Mr. West:

Our Chairman of the Board, Mr. Roberto C. Goizueta, has asked me to personally thank you for your letter. We are glad to have this opportunity to respond.

Coca-Cola and all our other soft drinks are wholesome beverages manufactured in compliance with the Federal Food Laws, the laws of all the states and the laws of more than 155 countries throughout the world where the product is marketed. The long history of use of soft drinks without adverse health effects further demonstrates the safety of our products.

We make no nutritional claims for Coca-Cola or our other carbonated soft drinks. In our view, every item in a person's diet need not be nutritional in the sense that it is "good for you" nutritionally. All of our soft drinks are marketed as beverages to be consumed for pleasure and enjoyment. We believe there has always been, and always will be, plenty of room in a balanced diet for consumption of pleasant soft drinks.

In response to your reference to our commercials using Jesse Jackson, I assume you are referring to the commercials of PepsiCo. with singer Michael Jackson. We are not affiliated with these advertisments in any way.

As you may know, the aim of our advertisements through the years has been to depict our products as being refreshing beverages enjoyed with good times, and to portray how they enhance any given situation.

Please know, Mr. West, that The Coca-Cola Company engages in a continuing program of research and development in cooperation with our advertising agencies. Different types of ads are considered in terms of consumer acceptance and all the factors that affect the purchasing decision of consumers. As this program continues, it is helpful to have the benefit of opinions such as yours.

Thank you, again, for taking the time to contact us.

Sincerely,

Patricia Martin
Consumer Information Coordinator

PM/sj

309-941 West 13th Avenue
Vancouver
British Columbia
V5Z 1P4

Royal Bank of Canada
1 Place Ville Marie
P.O.Box 6001
Montreal   October 12th 1984
Quebec H3C 3A9

For the attention of Rowland C. Frazee
<u>Chairman</u>

Dear Mr. Frazee,

        I made my pile the hard way in the construction caper,
through the now obsolete virtues of charging high prices, paying
low wages, and refusing to recognise the Unions, and I am now
expanding my interests.

        To this end I wish to acquire the controlling interest
in a major food processing corporation, the identity of which need
not concern you as yet, and consequently seek a bank of substance
to skilfully lead the project.

        Initially I considered engaging the services of American
Express, through my acquaintance with James Robinson and Sanford
Weill (do you know them?) but I suspect that a venture of this
type is outside their preferred field of endeavour, to your advantage
if you are able to convince me as to your satisfactory experience
in this area.

        I am obliged to write to you directly, as the banks out
here are staffed entirely by dizzy young girls (even the managers!)
and I wouldn't want to confuse their pretty heads with important
business matters.

        We're talking big money here, and I don't want to risk
a cock-up!

        If you feel competent to handle this undertaking with
despatch, perhaps you might forward your proposals for my personal
attention, which I will submit to my Board for full consideration.

                                Yours sincerely,

                                Bruce West

THE ROYAL BANK OF CANADA
HEAD OFFICE - BOX 6001
MONTREAL, P.Q. H3C 3A9

D. H. REINHARDT
ASSISTANT TO THE CHAIRMAN
AND CHIEF EXECUTIVE OFFICER

October 18, 1984

Mr. Bruce West
309-941 West 13th Avenue
Vancouver, B.C.
V5Z 1P4

Dear Mr. West:

In Mr. Frazee's absence on a business trip, I wish to acknowledge receipt of your letter dated October 12, 1984.

I have forwarded your letter to Mr. L.G. Edmonds, Vice President of our British Columbia Headquarters, in order that he is aware of your comments.

Yours truly,

THE ROYAL BANK OF CANADA

BRITISH COLUMBIA HEADQUARTERS
P.O. BOX 11141
1055 WEST GEORGIA STREET
VANCOUVER, B.C. V6E 3S5

October 29, 1984

Mr. Bruce West
309-941 West 13th Avenue
Vancouver, B.C.
V5Z 1P4

Dear Mr. West:

Your letter of October 12, 1984, addressed to our Chairman,
Mr. Frazee, has been forwarded to the Independent Business Group
for our attention.

The Royal Bank is the largest lender to business in this Province
and capable of effectively assessing any financial proposition
including your proposed acquisition of a food processing company.
We would welcome an opportunity to discuss this venture with you,
particularly as you are a client of the bank. As we were unable
to contact you by phone today, posibly you could give the writer
a call at 665-4025.

Yours truly,

B.F. Hann
Manager
Independent Business

309-941 West 13th Avenue
Vancouver
British Columbia
V5Z 1P4

Royal Bank of Canada
Box 6001
Montreal
Quebec H3C 3A9

October 31st 1984

For the attention of D. H. Reinhardt

Dear Mr. Reinhardt,

What are you people up to?

Your reply to my enquiry dated October 12th addressed
to your Chairman, informs me that he is away on a 'business'
trip, and that my letter has been forwarded to a Mr. L. G.
Edmonds, who is quite unknown to me, but is apparently
conveniently located approximately 3,000 miles from the
object of my interest!

For whatever reason alas I do not hear from Mr. Edmonds,
but instead from yet another new name, a B. F. Hann who has
discovered my private telephone number and has been calling me
with evident disregard for the confidential aspect of my enquiry.

In light of this extraordinary lack of propriety in
dealing with sensitive financial matters therefore, I have
secured more discreet usurers for my purposes.

Yours sincerely,

Bruce West

Copy to B. F. Hann

309-941 West 13th Avenue
Vancouver
British Columbia
Canada V5Z 1P4

Phil Donahue
The Donahue Show
2501 Bradley Place
Chicago
Illinois 60618
U.S.A.

October 11th 1984

Dear Mr. Donahue,

I'll come straight to the point. I am putting on a
television show here for a major sponsor, and I want you to
compere it.

I've been studying your own programme over a number
of weeks, and frankly I'm impressed!

You have created the perfect formula, three or four
atribilious lesbians ranting over trivial 'womens issues', and
a garrulous audience comprising bored housewives plagued by
gender identity crisis. It works every time and the mugs love
it!

Here's the plan. The show will be recorded in early
January '85, and my people will organise everything except the
Amazonians and the subject for 'discussion', which I shall leave
up to you.

I can guarantee a packed paying audience, who will jump
at the chance of a morning's respite from the supermarkets and
their 'exercise' classes.

What would be your fee Phil, and are you O.K. for
January?

As soon as I hear from you, my lawyers will submit full
proposals to your advisers, and we can start to make money!

I look forward to your early confirmation.

Kindest regards.

Yours sincerely,

Bruce West

                                        309-941 West 13th Avenue
                                        Vancouver
                                        British Columbia
Phil Donahue   Canada V5Z 1P4
The Donahue Show
2501 Bradley Place
Chicago   December 17th 1984
Illinois 60618
U.S.A.

Dear Phil,

        I'm amazed not to have heard from you regarding the
generous offer contained in my letter of October 11th.

        Not still thinking it over, surely?

        If you are not up to hosting our show, perhaps you
might have the courtesy to let me know. There is no shortage
of people in your line of work we can call upon for the job,
but we must hear from you one way or the other.

        I enclose a dollar to cover the cost of postage, in
case things are a bit tight at present.

                            Yours sincerely,

                            Bruce West

Enc.

                                        309-941 West 13th Avenue
                                        Vancouver
Phil Donahue   British Columbia
The Donahue Show   Canada V5Z 1P4
2501 Bradley Place
Chicago
Illinois 60618   February 15th 1985
U.S.A.

Dear Phil,

        Good Lord man, what's the hold up?

        We are ready to go here, and you are still
dithering over my offer of October 11th last, and further
reminder and down-payment of December 17th!

        I enclose a further two dollars to help swing
the balance - let's go!

                                        Yours sincerely,

                                        Bruce West

Enc.

Note: No reply received. --Ed.

309-941 West 13th Avenue
Vancouver
British Columbia
Canada V5Z 1P4

President Ronald Reagan
The White House
Washington D.C.
20500
U.S.A.

November 9th 1984

Dear Mr. President,

So! Another four long years in Office!

One hopes the predictions that your advanced years
might prevent your completing the full term will not come
to fruition.

Your critics should not underestimate the presbyopic
capability which so overwhelmingly engineered your successful
continuation in Office.

Having invested such generous quantities of energy,
guile and money hoodwinking the American voter into believing
that your proclaimed dedication to peace was likely to be
realised after the Polling Booths closed, it would be a blow
indeed if your untimely expiry was to preclude the opportunity
to disprove the popular conjecture that you will now initiate
a proliferation of invasions throughout the world.

To expedite your reply to this and my letters of
September 6th and October 10th, I enclose a cheque for $1.00
to cover the price of a stamp, on the assumption that even an
American President would not pocket a fellow's postage money!

Yours sincerely,

Bruce West

Enc.

THE WHITE HOUSE

WASHINGTON

November 21, 1984

Dear Mr. West:

Because the White House is prohibited from accepting monetary gifts or political contributions, we are returning your enclosure. However, the interest which prompted you to write is appreciated.

Sincerely,

Anne Higgins
Special Assistant to the President
and Director of Correspondence

Mr. Bruce West
309-941 West 13th Avenue
Vancouver, B.C.
Canada V5Z 1P4

Enclosure: Monetary item returned

309-941 West 13th Avenue
Vancouver
British Columbia
Canada V5Z 1P4

Central Intelligence Agency
Washington
D.C. 20505
U.S.A.

November 26th 1984

For the attention of William J. Casey
<u>Director</u>

Dear Mr. Casey,

     I am compelled to bring to your attention a matter of
extreme urgency which demands your immediate investigation.

     I have sent despatches to President Ronald Reagan on
three separate occasions, commending the stand of your Great
Country against our mutual adversary the Communist, even going
so far as to donate a substantial sum of money to the cause
with my last communication, and to date I have heard nothing!

     Sir, as an expert on National Security, does this not
strike you as very odd?

     I have no wish to interfere with the internal affairs
of your Nation, but you must agree that such strange behaviour
indicates that something is seriously amiss in the White House.

     In the interest of security, no doubt you will initiate
a thorough enquiry into the background and current activities
of the President, in order to flush out any proclivity toward
unconstitutional political leaning which may have previously
slipped through the CIA net.

     I await your full report in early course, and I will be
standing by in case I can assist with my evidence.

Yours sincerely,

Bruce West

309-941 West 13th Avenue
Vancouver
British Columbia
Canada V5Z 1P4

Federal Bureau of Investigation
Department of Justice
Constitution Avenue & Tenth St. N.W.
Washington D.C.   January 5th 1985
20530
U.S.A.

For the attention of William H. Webster
Director

Dear Mr. Webster,

        As a consequence of my involvement with top-level
international politics, during a recent exchange of
correspondence with President Reagan I uncovered what was
in my professional opinion, a Communist infiltration in
the White House!

        With no concern for my own personal safety and
reputation, I laid my life on the line and revealed my
findings in strictest confidence to William J. Casey at
the CIA.

        This was over six weeks ago, and the continuing
ominous silence from Casey, together with subsequent strange
noises from my personal telephone, leads me to suspect to my
horror that the rot may be more widespread than I at first
suspected!

        On the understanding that the FBI is above suspicion
in matters relating to the Eastern Bloc, may I entrust you
with the task of a thorough screening of the Casey fellow,
to discover if he comes up squeaky-clean in the Marxist
department?

        Needless to say, I shall delay exposing all to the
Press until I have the go-ahead from you. Mum's the word!

        I enclose a dollar for the convenience of your
postage, and await your further instructions.

                              Yours for a Communist-Free
                              North America,

Enc.   Bruce West

U.S. Department of Justice

Federal Bureau of Investigation

Washington, D.C. 20535

February 14, 1985

Mr. Bruce West
309-941 West 13th Avenue
Vancouver, British Columbia, Canada
V5Z 1P4

Dear Mr. West:

     Your January 5th communication to Judge Webster
has been referred to me for reply. I appreciate your concern.

     From the limited data you provided, there is no
indication that a violation of Federal law within the investi-
gative jurisdiction of the FBI has occurred. If you have
additional, more specific information which you believe would
substantiate a violation within our jurisdiction, please
do not hesitate to contact us. I can assure you that any
information you furnish will be given prompt consideration.

     I am returning the check you so thoughtfully sent.

              Sincerely,

              William M. Baker
              Assistant Director
              Office of Congressional
                and Public Affairs

Enclosure

Central Intelligence Agency
Washington
D.C. 20505
U.S.A.

309-941 West 13th Avenue
Vancouver
British Columbia
Canada V5Z 1P4

February 8th 1985

For the attention of William J. Casey
Director

TOP SECRET

Dear Casey,

        Evidently the alarming implications revealed in my
letter of November 26th have not sunk in, as you have yet
to summon me as a prime witness to your investigation of
the White House!

        More than likely you are still working under cover,
and I will be called to give evidence any day now?

        I can be on your doorstep at a moment's notice, and
to this end I enclose a dollar to cover the cost of the
postage of my Notice To Appear.

        Let's go!

                                        Yours sincerely,

                                        Bruce West

Enc.

Central Intelligence Agency

Washington, D.C. 20505

22 February 1985

Mr. Bruce West
309 - 941 W. 13th Avenue
Vancouver, B.C. V5Z 1P4

Dear Sir:

 Enclosed is your check for $1.00 that you recently
sent us in the mail.

 Please do not send us any money in the future.

Thaddeus P. Brockman

309-941 West 13th Avenue
Vancouver
British Columbia
Canada V5Z 1P4

Prime Minister Pieter W. Botha
Union Buildings
Private Bag X213
Pretoria 0001
SOUTH AFRICA

November 11th 1984

Dear Prime Minister,

May I convey my respectful sympathy to your Government
in these troubled times of renewed violence in your black
townships?

Don't be disheartened by ignorant opinion from abroad,
from weak minded liberals who take the view from the comfort of
their lounge-rooms that it is unreasonable for a native people
to be kept in low status isolation by the white immigrant
minority.

In my view it is an unacceptable impertinence for
citizens of foreign countries to criticize your hard pressed
security forces over matters in which they have no experience.
Under your excellent leadership, steady but positive steps are
obviously well under way towards the path of true demogorgon
democracy.

Here in Canada of course, the problem was prevented
from escalating by introducing the simple expedient of allowing
the native people to drive American built automobiles, and
providing unrestricted access to Government Liquor Stores, which
has maintained population growth at a minimum.

I am expecting confirmation this week of my appointment
as Chief of Police at Sudbury (Ontario), and prior to assuming
my duties in this capacity, I intend to take a vacation in your
delightful country, and I would consider it a great privilege to
meet you personally and obtain a first hand impression of exactly
the type of man you are.

Perhaps you could let me know if this would be possible?

Yours sincerely,

Bruce West

A.1/15/1

Union Buildings
Pretoria

1984 -11- 2 9

Mr B West
309-941 West 13th Avenue
Vancouver
British Columbia
CANADA
V5Z 1P4
C A N A D A

Dear Mr West

By direction of the State President I wish to acknowledge with thanks receipt of your letter of 11 November
1984.

The State President has taken note of your intention to
visit our country but, because of a very committed schedule and not knowing the dates of your intended visit,
it will unfortunately not be possible to accommodate you
regarding an appointment with the State President.

With kind regards

W P J EHLERS
PRIVATE SECRETARY : CAPT

/gm

309-941 West 13th Avenue
Vancouver
British Columbia
Canada V5Z 1P4

Liberace
4993 Wilbur Street
Las Vegas
Nevada 89119   November 15th 1984
U.S.A.

Dear Liberace,

      I very much enjoyed seeing one of your shows on the
television a few nights ago, and as I watched your richly
scintillating yet tasteful performance, I was reminded of my
childhood days, when my strange old maiden aunt with an unusual
predilection for rather sudden attire of habiliment like yourself,
used to entertain my fourteen brothers and sisters and I on the
Family Piano in the Drawing Room.

      You were indeed a most moving reminder of those nostalgic
years Liberace. My aunt of course has now thankfully passed away,
God bless her, and I wonder if I might beg an autographed photo of
you in your stage costume, to remind me of those odd, yet in a way
joyful years at the mercy of my beloved old relative.

      Thank you in anticipation, and may you continue to give
pleasure to millions for many more years.

                              Yours sincerely,

                              Bruce West

309-941 West 13th Avenue
Vancouver
British Columbia
Canada V5Z 1P4

Sir Robin Vanderfelt K.B.E.
Secretary-General
Commonwealth Parliamentary Association
Headquarters Secretariat   November 17th 1984
Palace of Westminster
7 Old Palace Yard
London SW1P 3JY
GREAT BRITAIN

Dear Sir Robin,

     My colleagues have suggested that my qualifications suit the
requirements for successor to your goodself for the post of Secretary-
General of the Commonwealth Parliamentary Association; it occurs to me
however that I may perhaps be over-qualified for the position, and
therefore request your guidance before formally putting myself up for
nomination.

     As you are probably aware, I act as confidential adviser to
various politicians and corporations on important issues of State
and International procedure. It is not my intention to unfairly
advantage myself by disclosing names at this stage, but suffice to
say I include Presidents, Prime Ministers, Bank and Corporation
Chairmen, and Police and Enforcement detachments among my obligations.

     It goes without saying therefore that I am well appointed at
the highest level of political and corporate involvement, and I also
have solid connections and extensive travel experience abroad,
particularly in South Africa, Chile, Argentina, Libya and Albania.

     I enjoy the benefit of dual nationality (British and Canadian),
am an excellent shot, and of course come up squeaky-clean with our
friends at Scotland Yard, Interpol, and the Royal Canadian Mounted
Police!

     Perhaps you might favour me with your opinion as to whether
the position would meet my high expectations, and I will gauge my
further action on your kind reply.

     In any case I anticipate being in London on business in mid-
December, and look forward to meeting you then, and discussing your
views further over lunch.

                              Yours sincerely,

                              Bruce West

From: Sir Robin Vanderfelt, KBE

**Commonwealth
Parliamentary
Association**

Headquarters Secretariat

Palace of Westminster 7 Old Palace Yard London SW1P 3JY Telephone 01-219 4666
Telegrams 'Comparlas Parl London' Cables 'Comparlas London SW1'

30.11.84

Dear Mr West,

I acknowledge receipt of your
application for the post of Secretary-
General of the Commonwealth Parliamentary
Association.

Yours sincerely,

Robin Vanderfelt

Robin Vanderfelt
Secretary-General

Mr Bruce West
309-941 West 13th Avenue
Vancouver
British Columbia
CANADA V5Z 1P4

COMMONWEALTH PARLIAMENTARY ASSOCIATION
CANADIAN REGIONAL COUNCIL
BOX 950
HOUSES OF PARLIAMENT
OTTAWA, CANADA

ASSOCIATION PARLEMENTAIRE DU COMMONWEALTH
CONSEIL REGIONAL CANADIEN
C.P. 950
EDIFICES DU PARLEMENT
OTTAWA, CANADA

February 25, 1985

Mr. Bruce West
309-941 West 13th Avenue
Vancouver, British Columbia
V5Z 1P4

Dear Mr. West:

Sir Robin Vanderfelt, Secretary-General of the Commonwealth Parliamentary Association, has asked me, as Chairman of the Canadian Regional Selection Committee to acknowledge and thank you for your application for the position of Secretary-General. Yours was one of a large number of excellent applications considered by the Canadian Selection Committee.

The regional aspect of the selection process has now been completed and I regret to advise that we have been unable to forward your name to C.P.A. Headquarters for consideration in the final selection process. On behalf of Sir Robin and the Canadian Regional Selection Committee, I wish to thank you for your interest in C.P.A. and extend best wishes for success in your future endeavours.

Yours very truly,

Arthur R. Donahoe
Chairman, Executive Committee
Canadian Region
Commonwealth Parliamentary Association

ARD:nk

309-941 West 13th Avenue
Vancouver
British Columbia
V5Z 1P4

Elmer MacKay
Solicitor-General
House of Commons
OTTAWA
Ontario
K1A 0A6

November 18th 1984

Dear Solicitor-General,

It is with a sense of gratification that I read in the Press you are in favour of re-introduction of the death penalty for murderers "in extreme cases".

Could you kindly elaborate upon your definition of "extreme cases"?

I take it this would include murderers of policemen, prison guards, and politicians? I also assume reciprocally that the same penalty would be applied to policemen, prison guards, and politicians who are convicted of killing innocent victims?

If this is so, then you will agree that a death sentence should be passed on Colin Thatcher, the MLA from Saskatchewan convicted of the murder of his former wife, as an example to the public that those charged with upholding the law are not exempt from their own legislation?

When the death penalty again becomes part of the Criminal Code, what form will it comprise? I have always considered hanging to be barbaric and out of touch with modern technology.

I personally favour the electric chair, as progressively increased voltage could be applied to the condemned man, which would have him hopping about like a prawn on a hot-plate for several minutes before succumbing, and if broadcast through commercial television to our homes, would serve as a sharp deterrent to perpetrators of serious crimes!

I await your views with interest.

Yours sincerely,

Bruce West

309-941 West 13th Avenue
Vancouver
British Columbia
V5Z 1P4

Elmer MacKay
Solicitor-General
House of Commons
OTTAWA
Ontario
K1A 0A6

February 8th 1985

Dear Solicitor-General,

What on earth's going on at your end?

On November 18th last, I went to the trouble of acquainting you with my suggestions regarding the re-introduction of the death penalty with particular reference to public executions via the Electric Chair, and I am amazed to record that I have yet to hear that my proposals have been adopted?

Here's two dollars. Put it towards the prototype Execution Chamber Fund, and let's get some public lynchings under way without further delay!

Yours sincerely,

Bruce West

Enc.

MAR 4 1985

Mr. Bruce West
309 - 941 West 13th Avenue
Vancouver, British Columbia
V5Z 1P4

Dear Mr. West:

I have received your letter dated November 18, 1984, concerning the reintroduction of the death penalty.

My personal view is that capital punishment should be available as a sentence for the most heinous cases of murder. I am sure you will understand that the definition of such cases requires careful consideration.

With respect to possible methods of execution should Parliament reintroduce capital punishment, I expect that all methods will be examined, in order to select the most humane one.

Thank you again for writing to me about this important issue.

Yours sincerely,

Elmer MacKay, P.C., Q.C., M.P.

309-941 West 13th Avenue
Vancouver
British Columbia
Canada V5Z 1P4

Procter & Gamble Co.
301 E. Sixth Street
Cincinatti
Ohio 45202
U.S.A.

December 6th 1984

For the attention of John G. Smale
President

Dear Mr. Smale,

       I am writing to express my profound satisfaction with
your excellent product, new 'Bounce'.

       We operate a large Kennels here, and since switching
all the dogs' diet to 'Bounce', we have observed a marked
improvement in several directions. In particular the animals
are of a more contented disposition, their coats are healthier,
incidence of fleas and mites have decreased, and breeding and
birth-rate are much improved.

       One small point however. As we use such large quantities
on a daily basis, I wonder if you could let me know where we
might be able to obtain a wholesale discount, as our feed bill is
quite substantial? None of our regular suppliers is prepared to
offer a reduction, but I'm sure a word from your good Offices
will swiftly bring them to heel!

       Thank you in anticipation, and should you wish to send a
team to make a television commercial on our premises, they would
be most welcome at any time.

                                    Yours sincerely,

                                    Bruce West

PROCTER & GAMBLE INC.

Post Office Box 355, Station "A", Toronto, Ontario, Canada M5W 1C5 Telephone 924-4661 Area Code 416 Telex 065-24170

February 26, 1985

Mr. Bruce West
309-941 West 13th Ave.
Vancouver, B.C.
V5Z 1P4

Dear Mr. West:

Your recent letter addressed to Mr. John Smale at Procter & Gamble
in the U.S. has been referred to me for a response.

Since our product Bounce is a laundry fabric softener in sheet form
for use in the dryer, I am somewhat puzzled by your enquiry. Is
there another product in the animal food field called Bounce, or
something similar?

Perhaps you could telephone me collect to clarify this.

Yours sincerely,

Barry J. Pipes
Manager, External Affairs

BJP:db

309-941 West 13th Avenue
Vancouver
British Columbia
V5Z 1P4

Procter & Gamble Inc.
P.O. Box 355
Station 'A'
Toronto   March 1st 1985
Ontario
M5W 1C5

For the attention of Barry J. Pipes
Manager, External Affairs

Dear Pipes,

        Good Lord!

        I am most grateful to you for explaining the
purpose for which 'Bounce' is intended, and you may rest
assured that our animals' diet will be corrected with
immediate effect.

        Thank you again for bringing this unfortunate
error to my attention!

                                    Yours sincerely,

                                    Bruce West

309-941 West 13th Avenue
Vancouver
British Columbia
Canada V5Z 1P4

Wm. Wrigley Jr. Co.
410 N. Michigan Avenue
Chicago
Illinois 60611
U.S.A.

December 17th 1984

For the attention of William Wrigley
<u>President</u>

Dear Mr. Wrigley,

Our laboratories have been conducting research in order
to identify the cause of a particular type of brain malfunction
which is demonstrating a serious increase in North America.

We were fairly accurately able to pin down the clinical
symptoms of our research, which include moronic staring through
glazed eyes, loss of thought co-ordination, inability to grasp
simple commands, extreme lethargy, lack of interest in
communicating, complete loss of ambition, and sharply reduced
speech participation.

For months we were baffled. All the information fed into
our computer proved inconclusive.

Then a breakthrough! It transpired that over 98% of our
patients were habitual users of chewing gum.

Astonishing though this at first seemed, we double checked
our statistics again and again, and the evidence conclusively
demonstrates that regular chewing of gum is isolated as the single
cause of the gross malfunction of intellectual capacity.

We will be submitting our Paper to the World Health
Organisation in early course, and prior to despatching same, we
would appreciate hearing your views on this alarming revelation.

Yours sincerely,

Bruce West

Wm. **WRIGLEY** Jr. Company

WRIGLEY BUILDING • 410 N. MICHIGAN AVENUE
CHICAGO, ILLINOIS 60611

Telephone: 644-2121
Area Code 312

WHOLESOME • DELICIOUS • SATISFYING

December 28, 1984

Mr. Bruce West
309-941 West 13th Avenue
Vancouver
British Columbia
CANADA V5Z 1P4

Dear Mr. West:

We're sorry and somewhat surprised to learn about your negative
attitude toward chewing gum.

Exercising the mouth and jaw muscles through chewing is a
natural instinct that can be traced back thousands of years,
to antiquity. The ancient Greeks, no slouches where civilization
is concerned, chewed the gum of the mastic tree, and the Aztecs,
whose sophisticated culture in Mexico's Yucatan peninsula
flourished a thousand years, raised the enjoyment of chewing
chicle from the native sapodilla trees to a fine art.

Here in America, the New England colonists began making spruce
gum at home 300 years ago, and gum has been commercially available
for more than a century. So I wouldn't become too concerned
about a world decline in intellectual capacity due to chewing
gum, though we agree with you that some folks do seem to display
a lack of old-fashioned common sense these days.

On the positive side, chewing gum helps relieve nervous tension,
eases monotony, provides a quick and convenient pick-me-up,
and is a handy, low-calorie substitute for cigarettes and
fattening snacks. In fact, chewing gum was considered such a
necessity that it was included in Army K-rations during World
War II as a welcome "taste of home" for U.S., Canadian and
British soldiers fighting in the trenches.

I hope the enclosed summary of facts will give you a fresh
perspective on a quality product we've marketed proudly for 92
years. And please enjoy the complimentary packages of Doublemint
gum we're sending you under separate cover.

With best wishes,

WM. WRIGLEY JR. COMPANY

Barbara Sadek

Barbara Sadek

309-941 West 13th Avenue
Vancouver
British Columbia
V5Z 1P4

Rothmans of Canada Ltd
1500 Don Mills Road
Don Mills
Ontario
M3B 3L1

December 11th 1984

For the attention of C. Landmark
Chairman

Dear Mr. Landmark,

    I wish to complain in the strongest possible vein over
your current magazine advertising.

    I have before me a full page colour advertisement for
'Rothmans SPECIAL MILD', which states in bold copy, "Great
taste...and they're mild."

    How on earth can a small paper cylinder packed with a
carcinogenic leaf, which is placed between the lips and ignited
for the express purpose of inhalation, possibly be accurately
described as producing anything other than a smell, and an
unpleasant, addictive and dangerous one at that?

    If you and I were in a small elevator together, and I
suddenly dropped my pants, bent forward and farted extensively,
would you in all honesty exclaim in delight, "Great taste!"?
I think not, and I trust you will take my point that the simile
is most appropriate to your grossly misleading advertising.

    Anyone who has had the misfortune to smell the breath
of the cigarette addict is only too aware that the stench could
most accurately be described as being close to dog excrement that
has been blended with vomit - perhaps as a 'responsible' company
Chairman you will consider using this more accurate statement in
your next campaign?

    Before I report your Company to the Advertising Standards
Authority, I shall wait to consider your defence of my points.

                              Yours sincerely,

                              Bruce West

Rothmans of Canada Limited

75 DUFFLAW ROAD · TORONTO, ONTARIO M6A 2W4

January 4, 1985

Mr. Bruce West
309 - 941 West 13th Avenue
Vancouver, B.C.
V5Z 1P4

Dear Mr. West:

We acknowledge receipt of your recent letter concerning the advertising of cigarettes. For your information, Rothmans of Canada Limited is a holding company not directly involved in the manufacture and marketing of tobacco products but in spite of this, we feel compelled to briefly respond to your letter.

Needless to say, we greatly deplore the examples and analogies used in your letter. They reveal a complete ignorance of the reasons why millions of Canadians use this product daily.

However, you are allowed in this free country of ours, to express your opinion and we respect that right. I would hope that you would do the same when it comes to cigarette advertising.

Yours very truly,

C.A. Denis

309-941 West 13th Avenue
Vancouver
British Columbia
V5Z 1P4

'Thrill of a Lifetime'
Box 9
Station 'O'
Toronto   December 12th 1984
Ontario

For the attention of Doug Paulson

Dear Doug,

          I watch your most entertaining television show every
week without fail, and may I say how much pleasure I derive
from it.

          My 'Thrill of a Lifetime' would be to be flown first-
class to Bangkok, and spend a weekend locked in a very small
room with a dozen young ladies covered from head to foot in body
oil, with whom I could reduce myself to an exhausted basket-case
at the end of the 48 hours!

          I should then like to be flown home (first-class of
course) under appropriate medical supervision, with a video
cassette of the vacation highlights to remind myself in my old
age of the generosity of your programme.

          In order to expedite the processing of my Thrill, I
enclose a deposit of five dollars, and look forward to receiving
a list of dates which would be suitable to you for this marathon.

                              Yours sincerely,

                              Bruce West

Enc.

309-941 West 13th Avenue
Vancouver
British Columbia
V5Z 1P4

'Thrill of a Lifetime'
Box 9
Station 'O'
Toronto   February 13th 1985
Ontario

For the attention of The Producer

Dear Sir,

        I have been sitting here with my bags packed since
December 12th last, when I sent five dollars to Doug Paulson
as a deposit for the expedition of my 'Thrill of a Lifetime'.

        How long do these things take?

        Will Mr. Paulson be sending me a receipt for my five
dollars soon?

        Please let me have your instructions by return of
post.

                                Yours in anticipation,

                                Bruce West

Editor's Note: CFTO-TV returned Mr. West's cheque but didn't tell him
              why.

309-941 West 13th Avenue
Vancouver
British Columbia
V5Z 1P4

The Seagram Company Ltd
1430 Peel Street
Montreal
Quebec
H3A 1S9

December 30th 1984

For the attention of Edgar M. Bronfman
Chairman

Dear Mr. Bronfman,

        Your name has been given to me as an entrepreneur of
substance and discretion with an eye for a bargain, and to this
end I am writing to offer your company the opportunity to purchase
my expanding chain of adult video stores.

        All our outlets do a roaring trade in renting and selling
the usual merchandise appropriate to a business of this nature,
but the real money is made from 'very adult under the counter'
sales (cash only - no receipts) which I know will immediately
appeal to a man of your obvious financial talent!

        Obviously a takeover of this vein cannot be negotiated
successfully in writing, and a personal discussion is therefore
indicated to hammer out all the facts and figures, so may I suggest
a discreet meeting at your Offices in order to get to know one
another?

        Unless I hear from you to the contrary, I will drop by
to see you on Wednesday January 31st at about 12.30, when we can
arrive at a mutually agreeable figure for this growing investment.

        I look forward to doing business with you.

                                        Yours sincerely,

                                        Bruce West

The Seagram Company Ltd.

1430 PEEL STREET, MONTREAL, QUEBEC, CANADA H3A 1S9

January 10, 1985.

Mr. Bruce West,
309-941 West 13th Avenue,
Vancouver, B.C.
V5Z 1P4.

Dear Mr. West,

        Your letter of December 30, 1984 addressed to the
attention of Mr. Edgar M. Bronfman has been forwarded to me for
handling.

        Thank you for bringing this opportunity to our
attention. However, we have no interest in pursuing this
opportunity.

                        Sincerely,

                        Arnold M. Ludwick,
                        Vice President, Financial Analysis.

AML/dw.

309-941 West 13th Avenue
Vancouver
British Columbia
Canada V5Z 1P4

Her Majesty Queen Elizabeth ll
Buckingham Palace
London S.W.l.
<u>GREAT BRITAIN</u>

April 16th 1985

Your Majesty,

        Will the Gutter Press never cease their hounding
innocent members of the Royal Family in order to increase
the circulation of their disgraceful Comics?

        The disclosure in today's papers that Princess Michael
of Kent is the daughter of a Nazi S.S. Officer, in my humble
opinion is an unpardonable infringement of the respect and
privacy to which your family should be entitled.

        Good Lord, we all have our share of skeletons in the
cupboard, why I myself have an uncle (twice removed) who is
a practising Socialist!

        Do I allow snooping reporters to blacken my good name
by revealing all in the working-class Media? No Ma'am!

        It is high time the Press was taught to behave with
greater responsibility when covering sensitive issues which
can confuse the less enlightened reader. I am quite sure
that Baron Gunther von Reibnitz was at heart just an ordinary
working family man, who enjoyed a relaxing evening in front
of the T.V. with the wife and kids after a hard days' interrogation
at the Office, just like the rest of us!

        Here's five dollars. Please use it to 'dissuade' Daily
Mirror reporters from overstepping the mark on any future
disclosures of this nature.

                        Your loyal subject,

                        Bruce West

Enc.

BUCKINGHAM PALACE

1st May, 1985

Dear Mr. West,

The Queen has commanded me to thank you for your letter about The Prince and Princess of Wales' visit to the Vatican. Any decision on The Prince of Wales' programme is taken by His Royal Highness. On the content of the programme, The Prince of Wales receives advice from many quarters, as was the case on this particular occasion.

I am returning your cheque for 5 dollars herewith.

Yours Sincerely
Robert Fellows

Bruce West, Esq.

BUCKINGHAM PALACE

2nd May, 1985

Dear Mr. West,

I must apologise for my letter of yesterday which, as you will have realised by now, was sent to you as the result of a mix-up in the large weight of correspondence which The Queen has received recently both on the subject of The Prince and Princess of Wales' visit to the Vatican and about the publicity surrounding Princess Michael of Kent and her family.

Her Majesty was grateful to you for writing as you did on the latter subject.

Yours Sincerely
Robert Fellows

Bruce West, Esq.

309-941 West 13th Avenue
Vancouver
British Columbia
Canada V5Z 1P4

Sikorsky Aircraft
N. Main Street
Stratford
Connecticut 06602   May 15th 1985
U.S.A.

For the attention of William F. Paul
President

Dear Mr. Paul,

        I am obliged to purchase a new helicopter as soon as
possible, as our present model has unfortunately been destroyed
through a misunderstanding with some over-zealous foreign
vigilantes.

        The new machine will be used primarily for the express
transportation of 'vegetable substances' in South America, and
must therefore be able to accommodate a payload of around 1,000
lbs plus pilot and two other personnel.

        Speed and low-level maneuverability are vital considerations,
as is availability in camouflage paintwork for mainly night flying
over rough terrain. Do you supply fixed armourments (two light
machine-guns should be sufficient), and what is the current quoted
lead time for delivery? I emphasise again that possession at the
earliest is of the utmost priority.

        Please send full details and prices by return post, for
my personal attention.

        I enclose five dollars to cover your expenses, and thank
you in anticipation.

                                Yours sincerely,

                                Bruce West

Enc.

**UNITED
TECHNOLOGIES
SIKORSKY
AIRCRAFT**

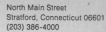
North Main Street
Stratford, Connecticut 06601
(203) 386-4000

June 17, 1985   IML-CAN-WED-85-0308

Mr. Bruce West
309-941 West 13th Avenue
Vancouver
British Columbia
Canada V5Z 1P4

Dear Mr. West:

In response to your letter of May 15, 1985 to Mr. Paul, we are pleased
to provide you with a specification and pictures of our S-76A
helicopter. This is the smallest commercial aircraft that we are
producing at this time. It is a 10,300 pound gross weight machine with
a useful load of 4,700 pounds. A review of the attached data will show
that the S-76 would meet or exceed your requirements. The fly away
price, depending on options and equipment, is approximately $3 million
in U.S. dollars. Delivery is established when the configuration is
determined.

At this time we would like to point out that we do not sell weapons and
that the end use of the machine would have to be determined before a
U.S. export license could be obtained. If this is a government
sanctioned operation, it might be more expeditious to have your customer
procure the helicopter.

Since we do not charge for marketing literature, we are returning your
check for five dollars. Thank you for thinking of Sikorsky to meet your
helicopter needs.

Sincerely,

UNITED TECHNOLOGIES CORPORATION

W. E. Drury/dhw

W. E. Drury, Jr
International Programs
SIKORSKY AIRCRAFT SALES

/dhw

SIKORSKY S-76 MARK II

UTILITY TRANSPORT

Certification:
FAR 29 Amendment 10 as an IFR Transport Category A helicopter.

Proven New Technology:
More performance with less maintenance and lower operating costs.

UNITED TECHNOLOGIES SIKORSKY AIRCRAFT

- **Twin Engines - Flat rated to 1000°, 90°F.**
  - Single stage centrifugal compressor - 8.5 to 1 compression ratio.
  - Engine turbine blade containment.
- **Main Rotor Blade**
  - High strength, non-corrosive titanium spar.
  - Non-linear high twist blade - greater lifting performance.
  - Swept trapezoidal tip - more speed with less noise.
- **Articulated Rotor Hub Design - Lower blade and hub stresses**
  - Elastomeric Bearing - eliminates hub lubrication.
  - Bifilar vibration absorber - reduces airframe stresses, maintenance man hours, and increases component life.
- **Tail Rotor Assembly**
  - Cross beam design - 2/3 fewer parts.
  - Composite graphite spar construction.
  - No feathering or flapping bearings to maintain or service.
- **Main Transmission** - simple 3-stage gear reduction system with dual lubricating pumps and redundant accessory drive system.
- **Flight Control System**
  - Fully independent dual hydraulic systems.
  - Dual hydraulic primary servo actuators with automatic by-pass and jam-proof servo valves.
  - Dual SAS/AFCS (optional equipment) components.
  - SAS FAA certification with one system inoperative.
- **Airframe Structure**
  - Multiple load paths, redundant structure.
  - Integral airframe-mounted auxiliary flotation (option).
  - Main Transmission structure designed to 20g forward, 20g downward, and ± 10g sideward loads.

Weights

Maximum Gross Weight	10,300 lb	4,671 kg
Useful Load	4,700 lb	2,131 kg
Standard Fuel Capacity	281 gal	1,064 liters

Performance

Maximum Speed	155 kt	287 km/hr
Maximum Cruise Speed	145 kt	269 km/hr
Best Range Speed	135 kt	250 km/hr
Single Engine Service Ceiling	5,200 ft	1,585 m
Maximum Range (30 minute reserve)	404 n.m.	748 km.
Fuel Consumption at maximum cruise	610 lb/hr.	277 kg/hr.

Seating Capacity

VFR Configuration	1 pilot
	13 passengers
IFR Configuration	2 pilots
	12 passengers
Executive Configuration	4 to 8 passengers

Dimensions

Main Rotor Diameter (blade tip circle)	44 ft. 0 in.	13.41 m.
Tail Rotor Diameter (blade tip circle)	8 ft. 0 in.	2.44 m.
Wheel Base	16 ft. 5 in.	5.00 m.
Passenger Cabin Length	8 ft. 1 in.	2.46 m.
Passenger Cabin Width	6 ft. 4 in.	1.93 m.
Passenger Cabin Height	4 ft. 5 in.	1.35 m.
Cabin Volume	204 ft.³	5.78 m.³
Baggage Compartment Volume	38 ft.³	1.08 m.³

Engines

Two Detroit Diesel Allison 250-C30S free turbine engines.
Ratings: Per engine, Standard Day, at Sea Level.

2½ Minute Power (OEI), S.L., 90°F	700 shp
Take-off	650 shp

PAYLOAD/RADIUS

Payload Outbound Only

Best Range Speed

No. of Troops @ 180 lb. (81.6 Kg)

Radius N. Mi.
Radius - Kilometers

OPTIONAL EQUIPMENT
- Standard S-76 Options
  - High Clearance, Fixed Gear
  - High Strength Self-sealing Fuel Tank
  - Armored Pilot Seats
- Planned Utility Options
  - Troop Seats
  - Cargo Floor
  - Low Pressure Tires

GENERAL ARRANGEMENT

309-941 West 13th Avenue
Vancouver
British Columbia
V5Z 1P4

Rod Murphy M.P.
House of Commons
OTTAWA
Ontario
K1A 0A6

January 26th 1985

Dear Rod,

    Regarding the advertisement for a Press Officer, New
Democratic Party - Parliament Hill, in today's Globe & Mail,
I think I can confidently claim to be the man for the job!

    In my capacity as a world famous author, I have
accumulated strong connections with the international media,
world leaders, political luminaries of all parties, corporation
executives, police and defence agencies, and various other
entertainers too numerous to mention.

    I am obliged to point out at the outset however, that
judging from close scrutiny of the performance of your Party
in the newspapers and on television, improving your image will
be an uphill struggle requiring some drastic grooming and
re-training.

    I recently had occasion to engage in correspondence with
Ed Broadbent (did you know he takes 4 months to answer his letters!)
and to be quite frank with you, I found his literary performance
lack-lustre in the extreme. Is he likely to be dumped in the
near future? If not, I fear there is much work to be done!

    I shall fly to Ottawa on Monday February 25th, and will
meet with you then to discuss details of my appointment, salary,
perks etc., at about 12.30 for luncheon.

    Unless I hear from you to the contrary I will assume that
this time is convenient to you, and look forward to making your
acquaintance.

                                Yours sincerely,

                                Bruce West

309-941 West 13th Avenue
Vancouver
British Columbia
V5Z 1P4

Dr. Susan Clark, Secretary
Presidential Search Committee
Mount Saint Vincent University
166 Bedford Highway
Halifax
Nova Scotia B3M 2J6

January 5th 1985

Dear Dr. Clark,

Reference your advertised vacancy for University President
in today's Globe & Mail, I am pleased to inform you of my
availability for early ordination.

Firstly, may I say how refreshing it is to note that your
University quite openly admits to catering for the special
learning difficulties women experience in higher education? If
more institutions followed your sensible and realistic example,
then the so-called equality movement would soon lapse into well
deserved obscurity, to the relief of all I am sure you'd agree!

Anyway, to business. My own background encompasses a vast
range of experience pertinent to university teaching, including
communication with governmental, political and religious leaders
world-wide, advising major corporations on various subjects, and
generally involving myself with all matters deserving of my
special attention concerning the problems of the twentieth
century lifestyle.

My latest book describing my experiences in these fields is
shortly to be published, and if any of the young ladies studying
at Mount Saint Vincent felt the need to discuss the content of
the text after hours in the privacy of my Rooms, I should be only
too happy to accommodate them.

I am incidentally, on first name terms with Prime Minister
Brian Mulroney, and also received a Christmas card from the
Premier of New Brunswick, Richard Hatfield.

As luck would have it, I shall be in Halifax on Monday,
February 4th, and I will drop in to run my eye over the Campus
and students, and discuss the terms of my appointment more
fully with you then.

I look forward to meeting you at about 12.30 for lunch
(on me!) on that date.

Yours sincerely,

Bruce West

309-941 West 13th Avenue
Vancouver
British Columbia
V5Z 1P4

Rod Murphy M.P.
House of Commons
OTTAWA
Ontario
K1A 0A6

February 21st 1985

Dear Rod,

As I haven't heard from you in reply to my letter of
January 26th, I am wondering whether to keep our appointment
on the 25th of this month as arranged?

I hate to rush you, but I have to make a decision soon
regarding whether to accept the post of President of Mount
Saint Vincent University, in Nova Scotia.

I know you politicians can be a bit cagey in the decision
making department, and I therefore enclose a dollar to encourage
an early reply!

Up the NDP!

Yours in anticipation,

Bruce West

Enc.

CHURCHILL

HOUSE OF COMMONS
CHAMBRE DES COMMUNES
OTTAWA, CANADA
KIA OA6

ROD MURPHY, M.P.

April 12, 1985

Mr. Bruce West
309-941 West 13th Ave
Vancouver, BC
V5Z 1P4

Dear Mr. West:

I want to thank you for applying for the position of Press Officer to the New Democratic Party Caucus.

I apologize for the time it has taken to respond to your letter. We received many outstanding applications for this position which made it particularly difficult to find the individual whose abilities best suited our very specific needs.

After a careful and lengthy evaluation, the interview committee recommended the hiring of Mr. Terence O'Grady. Mr. O'Grady has been employed as an information and press officer with External Affairs.

I will be placing your resumé on file with our Resource Office. Should you have further inquiries about other positions with New Democrat MPs please contact Kathryn Parsonage at 613-996-1911.

Yours sincerely,

Rod Murphy, M.P.

STITUENCY OFFICE
700
ATION ROAD
PSON, MANITOBA
N5

PHONE
OTTAWA: (613) 995-9732
THOMPSON: (204) 677-4588
TOLL-FREE RIDING:
1-800-442-0457

OTTAWA OFFICE
648S
HOUSE OF COMMONS
OTTAWA, ONTARIO
KIA OA6

309-941 West 13th Avenue
Vancouver
British Columbia
Canada V5Z 1P4

H. R. H. The Prince of Wales
Buckingham Palace
London S.W.1.
GREAT BRITAIN

December 22nd 1984

Your Royal Highness,

I was deeply disturbed to read in my paper this morning
that your sister Princess Anne, in a fit of pique, snubbed the
Christening of young Prince Harry in favour of a day's hunting
with that frightful husband of hers.

The pretext for this appalling display of manners is
ascribed to your not asking Her Highness to be godparent to the
young Prince, a decision incidentally which I wholeheartedly
endorse!

I don't doubt that in this age of declining standards
it is extremely difficult to select godparents of the high
calibre necessary to accommodate an heir to the throne, and I
am therefore pleased to respectfully submit my name for inclusion
on the godparent short-list.

For your interest, I am a loyal British subject of the
same generation as yourself, keen on hunting and fishing, have
a clean drivers' Licence and no police record, always vote
Conservative, and never wear a woolly jumper under a suit. I am
also on first name terms with Prime Minister Brian Mulroney (I
assume this is a plus!).

I would consider it a great privilege Sir, to receive
favourable consideration for this honourable duty.

I shall be in London in the New Year, as I have to discuss
my appointment as Secretary-General of the Commonwealth
Parliamentary Association with old Sir Robin Vanderfelt, and I
look forward to meeting Your Highness then, when we can discuss
Prince Harry's future at greater length. May I provisionally
suggest lunch on Tuesday January 28th? I look forward immensely
to your confirmation that this will be convenient to you.

Yours sincerely,

Bruce West

309-941 West 13th Avenue
Vancouver
British Columbia
Canada V5Z 1P4
H. R. H. The Prince of Wales
Buckingham Palace
London S.W.1.
GREAT BRITAIN

January 21st 1985

Your Royal Highness,

Further to my letter of December 22nd, I very much
regret that I shall have to postpone our luncheon engagement
for January 28th, as my meeting with Sir Robin Vanderfelt has
been adjourned whilst I conclude the delicate negotiation of
my imminent investiture as President of Mount Saint Vincent
University.

May I suggest we meet at the latter end of February,
at the convenience of Your Highness?

I enclose a self-addressed envelope for your expedience
together with a dollar to cover postage, and look forward to
receiving your confirmation of a time suitable for our meeting.

Kindest regards.

Your loyal servant,

Bruce West

Encs.

BUCKINGHAM PALACE

From: Equerry to H.R.H. The Prince of Wales

21st February 1985.

Dear Mr West,

    The Prince of Wales has asked me to thank you
for your letter of 21st January.

    His Royal Highness was grateful to you for writing
as you did and asks me to send you his sincere thanks
and best wishes.

Yours sincerely

Peter Eberle

Lieutenant-Commander Peter Eberle, RN.

Mr. Bruce West.

Mount Saint Vincent University

Halifax, Nova Scotia B3M 2J6   Tel. 443-4450

Board of Governors

April 12, 1985

Mr. Bruce West
309 - 941 West 13th Avenue
Vancouver, B.C.
V5Z 1P4

Dear Mr. West:

At a recent meeting the Presidential Search Committee established
a short list of candidates for the position of President.

Although your name was not included in the list, we should like
to thank you for your interest in Mount Saint Vincent University
and for submitting your application to us.

Yours sincerely,

Susan M. Clark, Ph.D.
Secretary
Presidential Search Committee

SMC/v

309-941 West 13th Avenue
Vancouver
British Columbia
Canada V5Z 1P4

The Kremlin
Moscow
U.S.S.R.

December 26th 1984

For the attention of Konstantin Chernenko
Chairman of the Presidium of the
Supreme Soviet of the U.S.S.R.

Dear Mr. Chernenko,

Like most western observers, I viewed the invasion of
Afghanistan by the U.S.S.R. some five years ago as a gross and
unwarranted intrusion of the worst possible kind.

Subsequently however, through the educational medium of
television corroboration, my eyes have been opened to the adversity
your hard-pressed forces are having to endure in their efforts to
maintain civil obedience in the hostile terrain of your unwilling
neighbours.

It is all too easy to criticise an army equipped with the
latest weapon technology from a country with a population of over
240 million, as they endure terrible hardships such as home-sickness,
vodka rationing, no television and who knows what other horrors, while
they relentlessly devastate their way through a small country with
a population of under 15 million, some of whom have the audacity to
defend themselves with rudimentary and antiquated small-arms!

Small wonder that tempers are running short in the Kremlin,
as despite the overwhelming odds, the handful of untrained Afghan
tribesmen continually thwart your crack troops, with losses on your
side dumfounding your Generals and causing loss of Military face in
the eyes of your critics.

As a small demonstration of my sympathy for your beleaguered
forces, I enclose two dollars. Buy the lads some woolly socks - I
should not be able to sleep at night for thinking of them catching
colds in those draughty helicopter gun-ships, as they dash about
here and there firing their lethal rockets at pockets of tribesmen
heavily armed with the latest clubs and sharpened sticks with which
to defend themselves and their families from your stabilising
influence.

Yours sincerely,

Bruce West

Enc.

309-941 West 13th Avenue
Vancouver
British Columbia
The Kremlin   Canada V5Z 1P4
Moscow
U.S.S.R.

                                         February 18th 1985

For the attention of Konstantin Chernenko
Chairman of the Presidium of the
Supreme Soviet of the U.S.S.R.

Dear Mr. Chernenko,

        Is there any foundation to the reassuring rumour of
your recent death, or at least, serious illness which is making
your appearances in public conspicuous by their absence?

        You will understand my natural concern, as I have not
received your reply to my letter and contribution of December 26th
last, and I therefore fear the worst.

        Perhaps you or your next of kin will be good enough to
let me know the current position?

        I enclose a further two dollars to go towards your
medical bills or funeral expenses, whichever is appropriate!

                                Yours sincerely,

                                Bruce West

Enc.

309-941 West 13th Avenue
Vancouver
British Columbia
Canada V5Z 1P4

The Kremlin
Moscow
U.S.S.R.

March 25th 1985

For the attention of Mikhail Gorbachev
Chairman of the Presidium of the
Supreme Soviet of the U.S.S.R.

Dear Mr. Gorbachev,

It is with a profound sense of relief that I find myself
able to extend a warm welcome to you as the new leader of the
Soviet Union!

One hesitates to speak ill of the dead, but I recently
initiated an enlightening exchange of important views with your
predecessor Konstantin Chernenko, whereupon the fellow unfortunately
passed on, which is frightfully bad form you'll agree? In an effort
to further the cause of harmonious East-West relations, I also went
to the trouble of including a couple of substantial financial
donations to the Cause, which I am saddened to report were not even
acknowledged by the Late Leader.

Not that one cares particularly about the money you
understand, but as a matter of common courtesy I should appreciate
your looking into the matter for me when you have a minute.

You may also be aware that I am a close personal adviser
to our Prime Minister, as the enclosed letter from Brian (Mulroney)
will demonstrate, and it is my pleasure Sir to assure you that
despite what you may have learned to the contrary, he is not a bad
type at all!

I look forward to hearing from you with regard to the
disappearance of my contributions to The Party through Mr. Chernenko,
and enclose a further five dollars to cover your expenses.

Needless to say, if ever yourself and the good Mrs. Gorbachev
are visiting these parts, it will be my privilege to entertain the
pair of you with a spot of tea on my Lawn!

Yours sincerely,

Note: No reply received. —Ed.

Bruce West

Enc.

309-941 West 13th Avenue
Vancouver
British Columbia
V5Z 1P4

Air Canada
Place Ville-Marie
Montreal
Quebec
H3B 3P7

December 29th 1984

For the attention of Claude I. Taylor
President

Dear Claude,

I have been seeking to purchase a suitable airline for
some months, and now that the Government has wisely decided to
get shot of Air Canada, I should be pleased to receive the
Prospectus for Sale together with current Balance Sheet by
return of post.

Having had the misfortune to be a victim of your
'efficiency' in the past, I am bound to say you are not at the
top of my shopping list, but I am confident that with some
drastic hatchet wielding, my Accountants will soon lick things
into shape.

All top management and executives will have to be
replaced of course, and complete staff re-training will be a
top priority.

With diligent pruning and efficient management, I see
no reason why Air Canada should not be able to operate like a
proper airline in very early course.

As an indication of my serious intention of acquisition,
I enclose a deposit of five dollars, which kindly receipt together
with early despatch of your Prospectus.

Yours sincerely,

Bruce West

Enc.

309-941 West 13th Avenue
Vancouver
British Columbia
Canada V5Z 1P4

J. Walter Thompson Company
466 Lexington Avenue
New York
N.Y. 10017
U.S.A.

December 29th 1984

For the attention of Don Johnston
<u>Chairman</u>

Dear Don,

       As you will probably have heard on the grapevine by now,
I am presently completing the final details of my purchase of
a major international airline.

       The airline in question is not held in high esteem by the
travelling public at present, and I therefore need an Agency which
is experienced at duping the masses into spending their money on
products they don't need.

       This is where you come in!

       Your Agency has been highly recommended to me in this
context, and for this reason I am able to offer you the opportunity
to come up with a viable campaign geared to bamboozle the mugs into
scrambling over one another to fly with us.

       This will be a unique occasion for your organisation to
acquire an enviable reputation in the advertising world, and make
a bundle at the same time!

       I shall be in New York in February, and I will drop in to
discuss this exciting project with you on Thursday 28th at about
12.30 for lunch.

       Perhaps you would be good enough to confirm that this
time will be convenient, and I look forward to doing business
with you.

                              Yours sincerely,

                              Bruce West

AIR CANADA ✳ PLACE AIR CANADA, MONTRÉAL, CANADA H2Z 1X5
CABLE-CÂBLE: AIRCANADA   TELEX-TÉLEX: 06-217537

OFFICE OF THE PRESIDENT
BUREAU DU PRÉSIDENT

January 28, 1985

Mr. Bruce West
309-941 West 13th Ave.
Vancouver, B.C.
V5Z 1P4

Dear Mr. West:

This is to acknowledge your letter of December 29th which was
referred to me for reply.

You are no doubt aware that Prime Minister Brian Mulroney
recently announced that Air Canada was not up for sale. We
must, therefore, decline your generous offer and return your
deposit cheque. I realize this will be a disappointment for
you, however, I do hope you will understand our position.

Yours very truly,

N. Duquette
Supervisor, Customer Relations

Enc.

309-941 West 13th Avenue
Vancouver
British Columbia
Canada V5Z 1P4

J. Walter Thompson Company
466 Lexington Avenue
New York
N.Y. 10017
U.S.A.

March 4th 1985

For the attention of Denis Lanigan
<u>Vice Chairman</u>

Dear Mr. Lanigan,

     I wrote to your Chairman, Don Johnston, on December 29th, offering your Agency the opportunity to pitch for a most lucrative and exciting campaign in the Travel business, and thus far I have yet to receive an invitation to your Offices to plan our strategy!

     I assume this to be an oversight by the Johnston fellow (not a very promising start, I must say), and to expedite your immediate response, I now enclose a dollar for postage and a self addressed envelope for your convenience.

     Let's go!

Yours sincerely,

Bruce West

Encs.

J. Walter Thompson

Denis Lanigan
Vice Chairman
Chief Operating Officer

J. Walter Thompson
Company

466 Lexington Avenue
New York NY 10017

212 210 7000

April 3, 1985

Mr. Bruce West
309-941 West 13th Avenue
Vancouver
British Columbia
Canada V5Z 1P4

Dear Mr. West,

Thank you for your letter of March the 4th, which
was waiting for me on my return from travels
abroad.

I am afraid that at the present moment we are not
able to work with you in the travel area and I,
therefore, return your check.

Yours sincerely,

/cl
encl.

309-941 West 13th Avenue
Vancouver
British Columbia
Canada V5Z 1P4

The Vatican
Rome
ITALY

December 30th 1984

For the attention of Pope John Paul ll

Your Holiness,

As the morals of the world continue to skate downhill like
a greased pig, it is refreshing indeed to listen to your iterative
pontifical bringing home to us the inspired words of syllogistic
rectitude.

As this planet teeters on the brink of starvation through
chronic overpopulation, you sensibly ordain abstention from the
use of contraceptives.

As millions of couples endure unbearable lives of relations
with their spouses at an end, you persist in refusing to recognise
divorce.

Truly your apostolic perspicacity is a blessing and a source
of comfort and relief to all men of reason.

There are wicked cynics among us who are of the misguided
opinion that an elderly celibate bachelor is not competent to be
charged with responsibility for the direction of the lives of
over 600 million Catholics. Naturally I do not number myself among
such misanthropes. On the contrary, I feel that you should go
further still, and ban the disgraceful activities which lead to
birth control and divorce, namely copulation and marriage!

I enclose three dollars. Slip into something less
ostentatious than your usual attire, and pop downtown incognito
one night and enjoy yourself. That should hopefully silence
unkind critics of your curious lifestyle once and for all!

Yours sincerely,

Bruce West

Enc.

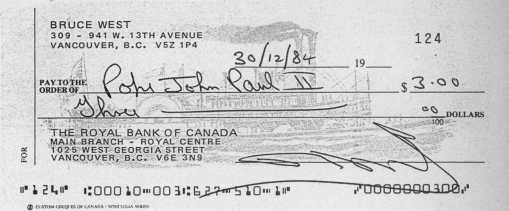

BRUCE WEST
309 - 941 W. 13TH AVENUE
VANCOUVER, B.C. V5Z 1P4

124

30/12/84   19____

PAY TO THE
ORDER OF   Pope John Paul II $ 3.00

   Three   ⁰⁰/100 DOLLARS

FOR

THE ROYAL BANK OF CANADA
MAIN BRANCH - ROYAL CENTRE
1025 WEST GEORGIA STREET
VANCOUVER, B.C. V6E 3N9

⑆124⑆ ⑆00010⑆003⑆627⑈510⑈1⑆   ⑈0000000300⑆

⊕ CUSTOM CHEQUES OF CANADA / NOSTALGIA SERIES

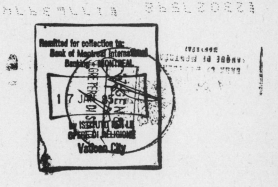

Remitted for collection to
Bank of Montreal International
Banking - MONTREAL

17 JAN 85

ISTITUTO PER LE
OPERE DI RELIGIONE
Vatican City

309-941 West 13th Avenue
Vancouver
British Columbia
Canada V5Z 1P4

The Vatican
Rome
ITALY

February 8th 1985

For the attention of Pope John Paul 11

Your Holiness,

        I see from my latest Bank statement/returned cheques
that you did indeed take my advice of the last paragraph in
my letter of December 30th, as my cheque was cashed by you on
January 17th!

        How did you make out?

        As you may imagine, I am a little disappointed that
you saw fit to accept my suggestion and donation without even
so much as a 'thank you', or even found time to comment on the
important theological issues raised in my letter?

        Perhaps you will answer my concerns when your busy
schedule permits, but in the meantime kindly forward a receipt
for my three dollars by return of post.

        Thank you.

                                        Yours sincerely,

                                        Bruce West

309-941 West 13th Avenue
Vancouver
British Columbia
Canada V5Z 1P4

February 10 1985

Commander Matt Koehl
National Socialist White People's Party
2507 N. Franklin Road
Arlington
Virginia 22201
U.S.A.

Commander Koehl:

     Since to Canada from my own country I have been
coming, I am missing greatly the rallies with my comrades
we are used to be having.

     And so I would like to be your Nazi Party joining
with your permission!

     From good Aryan family I am born; also have expert
shooting; in the next uprising am keen to be marching; and
in the head not entirely alright being.

     What are your uniforms having? Still mine I am
keeping from the old days!

     From you I will be hearing when it is possible
for me to meet for discuss of what is necessary to be done!

        Yours truly:

        B. von West

309-941 West 13th Avenue
Vancouver
British Columbia
Canada V5Z 1P4

March 25 1985

Commander Matt Koehl
National Socialist White People's Party
2507 N. Franklin Road
Arlington
Virginia 22201
U.S.A.

Commander Koehl:

What for are you to my letter February 10 not
replying?

This is not the efficiency we would be expecting
of the Commandant of a superior peoples!

I am now the urgent reply wanting, and here is
one dollar for the post stamp cost.

Yours truly:

B. von West

Enc. $1

May 1, 1985

B. von West
309-941 W. 13th Ave.
Vancouver, B.C.
Canada V5Z 1P4

Sir;

 We are not knowing what you with your letter of recent date
are meaning.

 We would therefore pleased be if you would to us be explaining.

Sincerely,

James Ring

P.O. Box 88
Arlington, VA 22210

Folk Art USA 22

B. von West
309-941 W. 13th Ave.
Vancouver, British Columbia
Canada V5Z 1P4

W.A.N.K.
309-941 West 13th Avenue
Vancouver
British Columbia
Canada V5Z 1P4

Billy Graham Evangalistic Association
1300 Harmon Place
Minneapolis
Minnesota 54403
U.S.A.

October 24th 1984

For the attention of Billy Graham

Your Reverence,

     I have long admired your sensible interpretation of
religionist epistemology, and the outstanding inculcation
with which your congregation is induced to contribute to the
expenses of your Church.

     In fact you have filled me with such inspiration,
that I have been moved to form a new religious order.

     It is called the West Atonement Neighbourhood Kinship
(W.A.N.K. for short, an acronym that rolls crisply off the
tongue you'll agree).

     I must emphasise straight away that under no
circumstances will our doctrine tread on the toes of your
fine Order. However, in the early stages of our development,
I would be very appreciative of any advice or assistance you
might be able to impart.

     A few old sermon scripts, cassette tapes of some of
your more puissant deliveries, or even just some details of
how to oil the wheels of a productive financial department.

     It goes without saying I am more than willing to pay
any charges you deem appropriate for your kind assistance.

     Many thanks in anticipation.

Yours sincerely,

Bruce West

P.S. Could you also oblige with a signed photograph of
     yourself as a personal memento?

1300 Harmon Place, Minneapolis, Minnesota 55403 U.S.A.
101 St. Andrew's House, Sydney Square, N.S.W. 2000, Australia
27 Camden Road, London, NW1 9LN, England
8 Villa du Parc Montsouris, F-75014 Paris, France
P.O. Box 870, Auckland, New Zealand
Incorporated—a non-profit organization

 Billy Graham EVANGELISTIC ASSOCIATION OF CANADA

Room 402—171 Donald Street; mailing address: Box 841, Winnipeg, Manitoba R3C 2R3 (204) 943-0529

November 9, 1984

Mr. Bruce West
W.A.N.K.
309-941 West 13th Avenue
Vancouver   BC   V5Z 1P4
CANADA

Dear Mr. West:

Thank you for your letter to Mr. Graham mentioning the new religious
order which you plan to form. Mr. Graham is currently away; therefore,
it is my privilege to correspond with you.

Since Mr. Graham will not be back to this office for a number of weeks,
he will not be able to share with you any suggestions he might have
concerning the establishment of your organization. We regret that he
cannot be of help to you at this time. Thank you for writing to him.

Sincerely yours,

Dr. Victor B. Nelson
Executive Assistant

VBN:mh

309-941 West 13th Avenue
Vancouver
British Columbia
Canada V5Z 1P4

Penthouse
909 Third Avenue
New York
N.Y. 10022
U.S.A.

March 22nd 1985

For the attention of Bob Guccione
Editor

Dear Bob,

I have just returned from a highly successful photographic
trip to the Bahamas, where I spent two months immortalising a
variety of exquisite models for publication in a quality magazine
of the Penthouse type.

The girls chosen for my Portfolio were of the highest
possible physical calibre, from Asia and Africa as well as
European stock, and besides the usual individual shots, I have
some rare 'group relationship' poses, together with some singularly
explicit exposures taken from the most unusual angles!

I know your readers will find my collection uniquely
stimulating, and the issue in which they appeared would be guaranteed
sold out on the first day they hit the news stands!

I shall be flying to New York on Tuesday April 30th, and
will hot-foot into your Office at about 12.30 to share my exciting
Portfolio with you!

I look forward to meeting you.

Yours sincerely,

Bruce de West

P.S. In the event of your considering the more unorthodox poses
to be more than your readers could handle, I am sure you
personally will derive great excitement from them in the
privacy of your own home!

Note: No reply received. --Ed.

309-941 West 13th Avenue
Vancouver
British Columbia
Canada V5Z 1P4

McDonalds Corporation
One McDonald Plaza
Oak Brook
Illinois 60521   January 3rd 1985
U.S.A.

For the attention of Michael R. Quinlan
President

Dear Mr. Quinlan,

As a frequent consumer of your fine gourmet comestibles,
I should be intrigued to partake of luncheon at the charming
establishment which features in your many television commercials.

The Restaurant in question is certainly a most attractive
looking venue, all the staff and customers are clean, tidy and
speak good English, service is prompt and courteous, and the
general atmosphere appears most conducive to agreeable digestion.

Why is it then that all your other outlets are such a
depressing contrast to the facility described above?

On the rare occasions when the serving staff are able to
speak or understand English, one cannot make oneself heard above
the cacophony as they scurry frantically back and forth behind the
counter screaming orders at one another at maximum decibels.

When and if the order is understood, invariably it is not
cooked and a wait is inevitable, defeating the object of patronising
a fast-food emporium in the first place!

Upon eventual receipt of one's order, sitting down to consume
same is an ordeal of unhygienic forbearance, as all available
seating is occupied by elderly men who have been sitting there all
day chain-smoking cigarettes and coughing incessantly.

Should one in despair resort to the drive-through service,
one is thrown into instant confusion, as the distorted and muffled
voice barely emanating from the order speaker is completely
unintelligible, sounding like a passable impersonation of a wasp
trapped in a cardboard box!

I look forward to your divulging the whereabouts of a
McDonalds which bears any resemblance to your advertised facility.

Yours sincerely,

Bruce West

RONALD L. MARCOUX
EXECUTIVE
VICE-PRESIDENT

January 28, 1985

Mr. B. West
#309 - 941 West 13th Avenue
Vancouver, B.C.
V5Z 1P4

Dear Mr. West:

Your letter dated January 3, 1985, addressed to Mr. Michael Quinlan has been referred to me.

The restaurant shown in our advertisements is in California, constructed on a site and used for the production of television advertising. This practice is commonly used by most advertising agencies in the development of their needed creative to support the media message.

The operation of our stores is tightly controlled to maintain a very high standard of what we call, Q.S.C. & V - Quality, Service, Cleanliness and Value, and although we don't hit the oustanding mark all the time in each of the categories, we sure try our best to be the best for our customers. So far, our customers have agreed with our high operational standards because, like yourself, they keep coming back again, and again.

Drive-Thru service has been well received by our customers resulting in a very high percentage of sales recorded in the Drive-Thru window. I think your analogy of the order speaker "sounding like a passable impersonation of a wasp trapped in a cardboard box", in some cases is a good one. The ongoing work to keep these speakers up to standard with the damp climate, vandalism, etc., certainly is a challenge to say it mildly. You can be assured that, sooner or later, we will find the solution.

In conclusion, all of our stores bear the resemblance of our advertised facility from the staff through to the constructed building. I wouldn't say everything is perfect, but I can assure you we work hard at trying to make it as close to perfect as possible.

I enjoyed reading your letter, and appreciate the time you spent as a good, concerned customer, helping to make us better.

Yours truly,

McDONALD'S RESTAURANTS OF CANADA LIMITED

Ronald L. Marcoux
Executive Vice-President

RLM/kg

cc: Mike Quinlan

309-941 West 13th Avenue
Vancouver
British Columbia
Canada V5Z 1P4

C/O William Morris
151 El Camino Drive
Beverly Hills
California
90212
U.S.A.

May 22nd 1986

For the attention of Joan Collins
<u>Superstar</u>!

Dear Joan,

    I witnessed you on television last night 'acting' in one of the ubiquitously tedious soap operas, and I have to say I was startled by your amazing resemblance to my late grandmother, who passed on only three months ago!

    Even more of a coincidence, as I watched your desperately vacuous performance, I detected the unmistakable twang of a London Cockney accent, from the very same City my dear old grandparent lived all her life! I continued to watch you in some fascination, mesmerised in nostalgia as I recalled those happy childhood days in the care of my London gran!

    I expect you have lots of grandchildren of your own Joan, and I know you will sympathize with my sad bereavement this year. Just think, it could even be that you knew my granny all those years ago in London, why who knows, you might even have been in the same grade at school together!

    Would it be too much trouble to ask for a signed photo Joan? It would be a welcome treasure at this sombre time, and I thank you kindly in anticipation!

Yours sincerely,

Bruce West

Note: No reply received. --Ed.

309-941 West 13th Avenue
Vancouver
British Columbia
Canada V5Z 1P4

The Pentagon
Washington D.C.
20301
U.S.A.   May 21st 1986

For the attention of Caspar W. Weinberger
Secretary of Defense

Dear Mr. Weinberger,

    As the U.S. Space Programme would appear to be on the brink
of lapsing into a permanent 'technical malfunction situation', I
am compelled to offer my condolences and perhaps a word of advice
here and there.

    It is a cruel irony that the recent miserable failures of
Satellite Launching Rockets, the Space Shuttle, Cruise Missiles
over Alberta (Canada), etc., have overshadowed the more notable
military successes which have made America the envy of the World!

    All too soon we forget the proud achievements of your
General Custer back in 1876, the defence of Pearl Harbor in 1941,
the war in Vietnam, the attempted hostage rescue in Iran under
President Carter, and of course the successful bombing of Libyan
civilians last month on the strength of Colonel Qaddafi having
conclusively been proved to have had possible connections with
terrorist attacks on European Airports.

    But, I digress! My purpose in writing is to avail your
technical staff of my valuable experience in matters relating
to the problems of mechanical flight.

    In my youth, I was a fanatical model aviator, and it must
be admitted that I also had my fair share of 'ongoing unscheduled
altitude loss exingency scenarios' (crashes)!

    In my case, invariably it transpired that the fault was a
lack of strength and/or longevity in the Rubber-Band driving the
Propellor, and, having studied the consistency of your recent
losses, I conclude that this simple solution to your problems
might well have been overlooked by your experts?

    Accordingly therefore, I enclose a Heavy-Duty Rubber-Band
for your people to test for suitability, and should this prove to
be the solution, I also enclose five dollars to purchase a good
supply of quality Bands for use on future missions!

    May you soon be back on target, developing much needed
sophisticated ballistics with the necessary capacity to annihilate
as many people as possible.

                                    Yours sincerely,

Encs.   Bruce West

OFFICE OF THE ASSISTANT SECRETARY OF DEFENSE

WASHINGTON, D.C. 20301-1400

PUBLIC AFFAIRS

12 JUN 1986

Mr. Bruce West
309-941 West 13th Avenue
Vancouver
British Columbia
Canada V5Z 194

Dear Mr. West:

   We are returning under cover of this letter your check for
$5.00, made payable to Secretary of Defense Weinberger, and the
rubber band which accompanied it.

   While we gratefully accept ideas and donations from citizens
who wish to improve the defense of our nation, it is indeed difficult to accept contributions from those who ridicule it. As a
result, we respectfully decline your suggestions and funds.

                          Sincerely,

                          Alice Tilton
                          Alice Tilton
                          Deputy Assistant Director
                          Defense Information Services Activity

Enclosures

309-941 West 13th Avenue
Vancouver
British Columbia
Canada V5Z 1P4

Ann Landers
P.O. Box 11995
Chicago
Illinois 60611   May 2nd 1986
U.S.A.

Dear Ann,

        I expect you're a keen movie-goer like myself, and I
wonder if you saw that great film 'Arthur' with Dudley Moore
and Lisa Minelli? Wasn't it funny? I really enjoyed it Ann,
and I'm sure you did too.

        The trouble is, ever since seeing the movie I have been
plagued by a recurring nightmare, which is now getting so serious
that my health is beginning to suffer. I'm too embarrassed to
discuss the problem with my personal physician, so I thought I'd
get your advice first, as you always come across as a sensible
old broad!

        The thing is, I keep dreaming that I'm having an affair
with Lisa Minelli! At first I thought it was my mind temporarily
playing a cruel trick on me, but now my health is seriously
deteriorating, as I find it impossible to get a sound uninterrupted
nights' sleep.

        I've tried every sedative I can think of to stop this
nocturnal torture, including hypnosis, sleeping pills, large
doses of Aspirin, counting sheep, even watching 'Dynasty', but
nothing prevents me from waking in a cold sweat with my heart
pounding in terror every night!

        Am I going out of my mind Ann?

        Will this terrifying ordeal cease in due course, or do I
need psychiatric attention?

        Please help!

                            Yours desperately,

                            Bruce West

ANN LANDERS

May 17, 1986

Dear Bruce:

So what's wrong with a little fantasy,
dear? Perhaps if you allow yourself to get through
one dream, they will stop haunting you. It's worth
a try.

Good luck and thank you for writing.

Sincerely,

Ann Landers

AL/ms

General Publishing Co. Ltd
30 Lesmill Road
Don Mills
Ontario
M3B 2T6

309-941 West 13th Avenue
Vancouver
British Columbia
V5Z 1P4

March 18th 1986

For the attention of Nelson Doucet
<u>Senior Vice President</u>

Dear Mr. Doucet,

At long last my eagerly anticipated tome <u>Outrageously Yours</u>
is ready to take the literary world by storm!

This fine work, it is probably safe to say, exceeds by a
considerable margin even the high standard by which an Author of
my standing is recognised, and I know you will have no hesitation
in luring me in your direction with a lucrative Contract and
substantial Advance!

As you will doubtless be aware, Armageddon Publishing of
Tasmania is poised on the brink of securing the rights to this
unique masterpiece, and I might suggest that swift action by
yourselves is the order of the day to avoid disappointment!

As luck would have it, I have an important business meeting
in Toronto on Tuesday, April 1st, and I should be able to fit you
into my schedule at about 12.30.

Have I got your address right, Nelson? Don Mills doesn't
seem to feature in my <u>1986 Dr. Livingstone's World Guide & Atlas</u>.
Perhaps it would be a sensible precaution to send your Best
Driver to meet me at the Airport; I should not care to be waylaid
prior to our concluding this important and historic Covenant!

Looking forward to seeing you on the First!

Yours sincerely,

Bruce West

GENERAL
P·U·B·L·I·S·H·I·N·G

March 23, 1986

Mr. Bruce West,
309-941 West 13th Avenue,
Vancouver, B.C.
V5Z 1P4

Dear Bruce:

Your March 18th letter is indeed good news for the general reading public.

We are happy to read that your forthcoming book exceeds your personal high standard and that Armageddon Publishing is eager to make you an offer. We strongly encourage you to become part of their list. After all, Tasmania is a natural market for your chef-d'oeuvre. Their recent bestseller "Fighting On" Vol. 16 shows their ability to sustain marketing enthusiasm.

Wishing you all the best in your new venture and thanking you for thinking of General.

Yours truly,

Nelson Doucet
Senior Vice President

GENERAL PUBLISHING
CO. LIMITED,
30 LESMILL ROAD,
DON MILLS, ONT.
CANADA M3B 2T6
(416) 445-3333
TELEX: 06-986664

EXCELLENCE IN PUBLISHING